I0568869

BENEDICTIONS GIVEN

To An Ordinary Woman

By

KRISTIN GEDSTAD

©2025 by Kristin Gedstad

Published by hope*books
2217 Matthews Township Pkwy
Suite D302
Matthews, NC 28105
www.hopebooks.com

hope*books is a division of hope*media
Printed in the United States of America

First Edition
Paperback ISBN: 979-8-89185-293-8
Hardcover ISBN: 979-8-89185-294-5
Ebook ISBN: 979-8-89185-295-2
Library of Congress Number: 2025943239

Remembering the days of Tinner and Tia.

And

In memory of Abbot David Geraets

Monastery of the Risen Christ, San Luis Obispo, CA.

And

Dr. Marie DiSciullo-Naples, Ph.D., SB Oblate and Spiritual Director

Monastery of the Risen Christ, San Luis Obispo, CA.

"*Benedictions Given to an Ordinary Woman* is a rare and beautiful memoir, written by a seasoned therapist who knows suffering from both sides of the chair. Kristin Gedstad, LPC, writes with the insight of a clinician and the soul of a seeker. As a fellow Licensed Professional Counselor, I was deeply moved by how she integrates faith, loss, mental health, and moments of divine encounter with stunning vulnerability and grace. This book doesn't just tell a story—it offers healing. Each chapter reads like a sacred reflection, reminding readers that God meets us in the quiet, the heartbreaking, and the mystery. A powerful read for anyone navigating pain, faith, or the long road back to themselves."

Jennifer Beasley, LPC
hope*writers Author and Certified Writing Coach.

"Kristin Gedstad is, first of all, sincere. Having experienced joy and heartache in her own life, filled with two marriages and two divorces, she also has children and grandchildren. She comes from a farm family with the stereotypical hard-working, honest, ethical, and genuine concern for the well-being of others. She now lives life as a single woman and is joy-filled as she has fallen in love with Jesus."

Jean Bearden, BA, Director of
Women's Ministries and subsequently on the
Senior Leadership Team of a large church for over 20 years.

"Kristin Gedstad spent 44 years providing psychotherapy, and in that role, she encountered every kind of problem and painful experiences her clients brought. Even though she describes herself as an "ordinary woman," she clearly has a history of extraordinary experiences, both professionally and personally. This book is about her personal experiences, but the thoughtful reader will see her wisdom and professional knowledge emerge between the lines."

Dr. Doug Anderson, PsyD in Clinical Psychology,
MA in Clinical Psychology, MA in Counseling, MDiv.

Table of Contents

Foreword

Most people hope and strive for a successful life that may manifest in a financial, interpersonal, and/or professional way. Depending on our individual goals, interests, and ambitions, we put forth a great effort to accomplish the steps needed for these successes to be realized. In the following pages, Kristin shares her success story. Her valiant efforts of striving, aiming high, and by all appearances making her mark in her professional life as a Licensed Marriage & Family Therapist (LMFT), in her family life as a spouse to her husband, a mom to her children, a daughter to her mother and father, and a granddaughter to her grandma, "Nemo." She was also "bringing home some of the bacon," which allowed her a lifestyle for her and her family that she was enjoying with them.

Then, like the shell of Humpty Dumpty, something cracked, and Kristin began her great fall from her many successes into the hands of the true and living God. Her journey shift began with her not being able to see very well anymore. She was devastated! When faced with a brokenness and vulnerability so raw and far from what is our familiarity, this would be the reaction of most of us. And, like Kristin, we would do almost anything to return us to our comfort zones; our sight, our marriage, and to be with our loved ones forever. We would fight to recover how things have always been until we AWAKEN and realize there is nothing left for us to do except surrender ourselves to God's will. In Kristin's journey, her initial surrender is to the prayers of others in proxy for her, and when she does, she receives complete healing of her eyes, and her eyesight is restored. She surrenders her significant relationships despite her reluctance and uncovers her call to be an instrument of God's love for others. She lets go of her self-consciousness, risking "what will others think of her," and as a woman of faith, experiences the awareness of God's will in her life each day.

This is a journey of a life-faith experience that demands and costs all that is not in our control, and **that is everything!** It is a daily surrender to God's unconditional love, forgiveness, and mercy that's available to all of us. Yes, these are Kristin's stories, her journey, as well as our stories and our journey. It is the miraculous story of the healing of eyes that releases the grace for the vision to see that Jesus Christ is Lord, and without that vision, we will indeed perish!

> "Where there is no revelation, the people cast off restraint; but happy is he who keeps the law."
> Proverbs 29:18, NKJV, Emphasis Added

Dr. Marie J. Disciullo-Naples,
Ph.D., SB Oblate and Spiritual Director

"If only I may grow:
firmer, simpler – quieter, warmer."

Dag Hammarskjöl

About Good and Evil
By Jean Bearden

A s you read these Benedictions, you may be surprised by some of the experiences described. Yet, it calls to mind the words of Christ, who said, "You will know them by their fruits"(Matthew 7:20, NASB). If you look carefully at the results or outcomes of these visitations, you will see that each one solidified the truth for Kristin that God in the persons of the Father, Son, and Holy Spirit exists. And this, in someone who wasn't even looking. Even more, knowing Kristin as I do, the fruit expresses itself through her life in generosity, love, peace, humility, and more. She has been profoundly changed.

Before judging this one woman's rather unusual experience, re-member, (or maybe hear it for the first time) God's story given to us as the Bible tells us God used Cyrus, a non-believing ruler to restore God's people to their land; a donkey to warn Balaam to be careful; a fish to turn Jonah around; and an unmarried virgin woman to bear a son. God doesn't always do what we expect God to do. What we do expect, however, is good fruit from whatever God does and however God does it. These benedictions will truly bless you if you come to recognize, as Kristin did, the workings of a magnificent and unlimited God. The God who desires to bless you.

Jean Bearden holds a BA from Augustana University, ten years as Director of a Women's Ministry, and twelve years on the Senior Leadership Team of a large two campus church. Currently active in her church and enjoying retirement with her husband and loving on her grandchildren. Jean and Kristin attended college together at Augustana University, in Sioux Falls, South Dakota. She has been a close friend of Kristin's since that time.

PREFACE

As a child, listening, encouraging, and helping others always came naturally to me. My innate skills have been enhanced, shined and polished through years of education and 44 years as a Licensed Professional Counselor LPC, Licensed Marriage and Family Therapist LMFT, Qualified Mental Health Professional QMHP, and Licensed Social Worker LSW.

I want to say something important to you before you get into this spiritual memoir. If anything in this book triggers you, please call the National Mental Health Hotline at 988, text 741741, or 24/7 assistance at 866-903-3787. You can also call NAMI (National Alliance on Mental Illness) at 1-800-950-6264. It may be helpful to speak to someone at a church or contact/Google a local mental health agency/therapist in your area.

Professionally, it's been my job to sit in the background of other people's lives and carefully listen. Then I verbally gave them back to themselves in ways they may not have seen or thought of due to their emotional pain. Together, we would explore alternative ways they could help themselves.

I was a caretaker. I've never been a leader or someone who dares to stand alone for a cause. I've always been a good support person, a first-rate background person. I know this about myself. I've never been a risk-taker. Sharing my innermost personal spiritual experiences with you is no small task for me. At 71 years of age, I felt I could no longer sit on "This Little Light of Mine," so "I'm going to let it shine!"

INTRODUCTION

I am a person of faith, truth, and integrity. I have no idea why God shared these spiritual experiences with me. My spiritual director, Dr. Marie, said it's because God loves me. If I were to guess, I'd say yes, God loves me, and maybe God gave them to me when He knew my human spirit needed them. These experiences helped me to simply go on living. I was depressed, to varying degrees, about my marriage for a very long time. Or maybe I'm to share them with you, the reader? Perhaps you chose this book because you were searching too, as was I. As I did. Either way, once I'd experienced the Divine, everything else dropped away, and I only wanted to be with Jesus. There is nothing left for me to desire on this earth and no one I'd rather belong to.

As I've spent time in the Bible reading God's holy word, I have found the words become more than just words on a page. In fact, the words were inviting, soft, restful, comforting, and peaceful. Figuratively speaking, I could lay my head down upon God's words and feel quenched and completely full of God's love and graciousness.

It has been my hope that this memoir will be helpful to you as you read about the spiritual experiences that have saved me as I have navigated my way through this human life, listening for those quiet nudges that are the Holy Spirit's way of leading us towards something good. For only good comes from God, Jesus, and the Holy Spirit.

For a long time, perhaps 15 years, I lived on a fast track. I was a counselor. I was a graduate student. I was a married-but-single-parent, and I exercised regularly. I kept up with my friends, I taught the 7th grade Human Sexuality Course at our church's Sunday School. For three years, I was the Church Council President. I cooked, I cleaned our home, I washed our clothes, and I took care of our two children. I didn't want to miss a minute of fun! I also had times when I struggled with Clinical Depression and Anxiety. Depression is a mental health issue. It runs deep in my family, much like a river that carves through flat lands, making itself at home while quietly unraveling everything around it.

My depression began in my teens. I was introduced to it as a young girl as I watched my maternal Grandmother trudge up the stairs and crawl into the bed in my room, where she and Grampy would stay for their two-week visit every summer and Christmas. They lived in Janesville, Wisconsin, which was a 500-mile drive they made twice a year. I would peek through a crack in my bedroom door and watch as my grandma lay down on the bed, turn her face to the wall, and cover her head with a blanket. That was when I knew I had what she had. I didn't know what it was called or if it had a name, but I felt her internal heaviness. I knew that it matched my own, an internal darkness that held me down. Later in life, as I studied to become a social worker and a counselor. I learned this was a low-grade depression. The internal weight on my soul was called Dysthymic Disorder. A low-grade, chronic, chemical imbalance in my brain. My depression increased in my postpartum years as my mind struggled to adjust to two beautiful children who were mine. I was unable to drive as I feared someone would crash into my car and hurt my babies. I even worried when they started to crawl and thought I needed to also crawl on top of them, should the ceiling fall down. My Dysthymia (when DSM IV was used) continued into my early 20s when I married my husband. My Dysthymia became Major Depression (DSM IV) during the struggles in my marriage.

In my early 20s, I wore suits, pumps, and carried a briefcase. I had a serious job as a social worker and counselor. I intended to be taken seriously. I believed I was in control of my life. I'd worked hard to gain the respect of others as a competent counselor and sign language interpreter. I was very proud of all of my accomplishments!

Potential clients called to request me as their counselor, and I was honored. My employer took me to lunch to ask if I was happy. I was! The agency's administration loved me because I was bringing in more money as a part-time staffer than some of the full-time staffers. I was at the top of my game!

I finally thought I was on solid ground. But my world started to dim, literally. My vision was blurring/fogging, and everything started to slip. Suddenly, I'd lost my sense of control over my life, the structure that kept me sane, the belief that if I tried to live a good Christian life, I would be safe from all the ills of the world and be in charge of my own destiny. I didn't understand what was happening to my body, but I was about to find out.

CHAPTER 1

The Healing

FALL 1988

I'm from a family of secret-keepers. We did not talk about our ailments, so my decision not to tell anyone about losing my eyesight was nothing out of the ordinary; it was our family norm to keep one's business to oneself.

In 1988, a year after my vision started to fade, I was diagnosed with Adie's Tonic Pupil, a degenerative, neurological eye condition that at times affected young women but primarily affected women in their seventies and eighties. I was thirty-four years old, and I could barely see. I had been referred to a specialist in town by my regular optometrist, who, on that day, grew quiet during my yearly exam. I was, at times, seeing double vision. My eyesight had become increasingly blurry. He usually talked a lot and would be a jokester, but on this examination date, he had grown increasingly quiet. There were no jokes that time. He asked questions, and I answered them.

When he mentioned what ophthalmologist he was referring me to, I felt afraid. I knew this doctor had a reputation as an excellent Doctor, and he was only referred to when one's eyesight was really bad. When I saw the ophthalmologist, he diagnosed the condition as Adie's Tonic Pupil. He said my eyes would become progressively worse as I grew older and prescribed trifocals, which is a corrected step up from bifocals. I was devastated. My world as I knew it spun out of control; the ego structures I had lived by, especially the notion that "I am in charge of my destiny," no longer held me up. I no longer understood what was happening to me. I wanted to understand and go back to the way it was before, and yet my body, as I had known it, had changed and left me vulnerable and afraid.

Yet, after a few months, I was still unable to accept the doctor's diagnosis, so I made another appointment with him, hoping he'd discover he had made an error. Though I already knew this particular doctor didn't make errors. He was known to be the best eye doctor in the area, and his assistant told me he didn't like being challenged, but I wanted him to re-examine my eyes, so his receptionist hesitantly worked me in. The doctor was brisk while he re-examined my eyes. The diagnosis came back the same. I was crying. I wanted to cling to the doctor's white coat. I wanted him to tell me it would be alright, that he could fix my eyes somehow, but he didn't do that. He was a busy man, and he exited the room telling me in a firm, matter-of-fact way that I "needed to adjust to the change in my vision, the increased blurriness, and seeing double vision." I was sobbing as his assistant entered the examination room and kindly helped me out of the chair and to the front door.

The idea of being blind was something I had thought about and feared greatly. I was an interpreter for the deaf, and being hard of hearing or deaf didn't scare me like the thought of blindness did. I couldn't handle the thought that others would pity me if they knew about my inability to see. Being vulnerable to others was more than I could fathom, so I didn't tell anyone except my husband and my mother. I was a secret keeper.

My fear of not being able to see propelled me to try harder to live life as if I could see. I purchased the most difficult piano rendition of "Canon in D" by Pachelbel. I loved this piece, and I learned to play it to near perfection. I used a magnifying glass to write all the notes in big, bold print until I'd memorized the piece by heart. I played this piece repeatedly. I played louder when I cried, I played harder when I was angry, and I played it during times of emotional unrest. Keeping it a secret and mastering a piano piece of that magnitude was the only way I knew to deal with my fear of blindness. My way of coping with the situation, I believe, was that a certain degree of denial sustained me emotionally, as I thought if I were truly blind, I'd be unable to play this piece, even though I had written all the notes out in bold print.

Coincidentally or not, this was a dark time in my life, filled with personal and spiritual drifting. My mother and Saint John of the Cross would describe it as a "dark night of the soul." Another secret I was holding from the family was the reality that I lived in a loveless marriage. The toxicity of my loveless commitment added to the degeneration of my physical health, my emotional well-being, my spirit, and the essence of who I was. My "dark night of the soul," along with my failing eyesight, seemed to become darker each day. Then, at my most vulnerable, an unexpected light turned on.

In 1989, my mother attended a month-long retreat at a Benedictine Monastery in Pecos, New Mexico, led by Abbot David Geraets, O.S.B. One evening, my mom called me from the Pecos Monastery to ask if she could sit in as a proxy for me during a healing service that was scheduled for that evening. Mom and Dad were Lutheran and raised us three children in a conservative Lutheran household, but they believed that regardless of our Christian labels, God bestows His love on all his children. Abbot David had the charism of healing, and particularly the specific gift for healing of the eyes. Unsure how to respond to this unexpected request, I said, "Sure, if you want to." Of course, I believed in God; I always had. However, I never expected anything to come from this offer, though I was thankful for her generous thought, I quickly forgot about it. I had other things on my mind. Desert Storm was ramping up, and this weighed heavily upon my heart as many of my clients had spouses who had been called to serve in Iraq. My brave but struggling clients, alone, home with their children, single parenting, holding down two jobs, along with all the other stresses that had previously been shared by two, deeply saddened my heart. And to a large degree, I identified with my clients, as I too was a married-but–single–parent and I too had to deal with life on a daily basis, alone.

The next day, while driving home from a second job in Sioux Falls, South Dakota, I started to pray. I often do this when driving. As I prayed, I was overcome with the most altruistic feeling I have ever had. To this day, I have never had such selfless feelings, feelings that contained such depth and concern for others, nor could I have imagined the profound intensity of my altruism. I was completely unselfish. I prayed for the safe return of my clients' spouses and the cessation of war. In exchange, I gladly gave up my desire for improved vision in favor of the war to desist for the larger good of others and the world. It was a small gesture for a big war, yet it was all I had.

I wiped my face and eyes clear of tears, and in doing so, it seemed my vision was somehow different. I was too afraid to dwell on it, fearing it was becoming worse. I chalked up the blurriness I was experiencing as normal for tear-stained and strained red eyes that had been crying for nearly an hour. However, on the drive home, I kept taking my trifocals off and putting them on again. I wasn't sure what I was sensing, but it seemed I could see better without them. I was too afraid to hope for anything, and this hope seemed to be far too bizarre to be real. I'd had no experience with miracles. While I believed, I never considered that a miracle would happen to me.

The next day, my mom called to inquire about my eyesight and whether I had noticed any changes in my vision. I was hesitant to tell her I feared my vision had become worse, as my trifocals (which are stronger than bifocals) seemed to increase the blurriness. However, she encouraged me to see another ophthalmologist to re-evaluate my eyes. Once again, I was hesitant; I didn't want to hear that diagnosis again, and I didn't want to be coldly dismissed like I was at the first diagnosis of Adie's Tonic Pupil. Finally, I agreed to go, though I suspected my fear had already come true. I feared my eyes had become worse; after all, I reminded myself, it was a degenerative disease. I decided to find a local ophthalmologist in Brookings. When I saw him, he kindly inquired about my vision and why I wore trifocals. I explained my previous diagnosis, and he began to review my chart that I had sent to him. He began his examination of my eyes: I was nervous. His assistant came and went at his request. I felt anxious because nobody was saying anything to me. I asked the doctor a question about my vision, but he asked me to wait until he had completed his entire examination. His response added to my anxiety, but I sat still and wide-eyed while looking into the bright light of those big machines, waiting. Upon the conclusion of his examination, the ophthalmologist turned away from me and again consulted my file. I felt dreadfully uneasy at that moment. I assumed he was gathering his information and thoughts as to how he was going to tell me my eyes had become worse. Then, he swung his chair directly in front of mine and, moving the big eye instrument aside, he looked straight into my eyes and told me, "I find absolutely no symptoms of Adie's Tonic Pupil." He said my eyes were not only healthy, but my vision was very good! He wrote out a prescription for regular lenses and told me I was probably several years away from even needing bifocals. I was stunned and speechless. I wanted to tell him about Abbot David and the healing service, about my mother who sat in proxy for me for my eyes, but I was too embarrassed to say anything. After all, it was unbelievable! Besides, I worried about what he would think of me. I didn't want to sound as unstable as this entire situation seemed, so I said nothing at all, thanked him for his kindness, and left feeling very shaky.

The drive home was surreal. I was numb and in shock. I felt as if I should jump out of my car, kneel in the street, and give thanks to God for restoring my vision, but of course, I couldn't do that in moving traffic. Instead, I continued driving with feelings of strangeness, astonishment, and disbelief whirling within me.

When I entered our home, I found my husband sitting in his chair reading the newspaper. I wondered how I could tell him my news without sounding as if I'd lost my mind, but I couldn't come up with a way, so I just blurted it out. "My eyes have been healed; I no longer have Adie's Tonic Pupil!" This reported miracle must have come as quite a shock to him, as he calmly said, "Well, that's great, Kris." "Yes!" I responded, "It is great!" and I went into our bedroom and stood in silence for a long time.

Finally, at my bedside, I got down on my knees and prayed my prayer of humble thanksgiving. As I prayed, I felt that my prayer sounded so small and insignificant compared to the miracle I had received. I felt I wasn't being grateful enough; still, receiving a miracle was something I didn't know how to integrate into my mind or my life, and saying "Thank you, God," to the One who created the universe sounded so minute, so unworthy. What I really wanted to do was host a party of praise! I wanted to call all my friends and celebrate God's great gift to me. I wanted to hear horns tooting and people singing, I wanted to shout my thankfulness from my rooftop. I wanted to stop traffic with the good news, but I feared my friends would think I was out of my mind. What if they didn't believe me anyway? I hadn't confided in anyone. I'd never told any of my friends or the rest of my family about my eye condition. How could I expect them to believe me and celebrate this miracle with me? No, I wouldn't say anything. So I, the secret keeper, remained kneeling, saying my small thanks to God as I tried to absorb the joy and celebration I felt in my heart. Yet, my heartfelt thanksgiving still felt immensely small and insufficient within me.

The next day, I called Mom to tell her what the doctor had said. She was overjoyed! Later that evening, she called me again with a message from Abbot David. I was amused by what Abbot David had told Mom, "Her life will never be the same," he said. I was perplexed by what Abbot David said. I'd never met him, and I had no idea what his statement could mean. I was tremendously grateful, but I was still in shock. Whenever I feel awkward in a situation, I hide my emotions behind humor, so I said, "Gosh Mom, if I'd known this was really going to work, I'd have had you throw in my TMJ (a jaw disorder) too!" Then, more seriously, I asked Mom to tell Abbot David, "Thank you for healing my eyes, and I hope to meet him one day." My message of thanks to Abbot David again sounded minuscule when voiced compared to the immeasurable gift I'd received. A few weeks later, Mom returned from the monastery and reminded me it wasn't her or Abbot David who gave me my miracle; it was God working through them.

Months later, I learned the ophthalmologist in Brookings, who confirmed that my eyesight was very good, was a missionary and had spent a year in our small town for recertification before returning to a third-world country to provide medical care to the eyes of the poor. Now, I really wished that I had taken the risk and told him about Abbot David and the healing service to restore my vision, suspecting he would have understood as a Christian and believed me.

"Praise the Lord, my soul, and forget not all his benefits—
who forgives all your sins and heals all your diseases."

Psalm 103:2-3

THOUGHTS

Looking back, I recall how stunned I was when I realized I do not have control over my own life; God does! It was an earth-shattering moment for me. This came as quite a shock, as I had always believed I was in charge of my life. I had believed that if I worked hard, was kind to others, and lived a life as a Christian, I would achieve my goals. It never dawned on me that something I didn't plan could enter my life, let alone devastate me. I now believe that I do not own my life; God does, and God gave me life so that I might do something with it, something for the good of others in the world. I am called to look after my brother and sister. I am called to be a counselor, to listen and to help others help themselves, not to just focus on me and my little world that I thought was so big and important. I believe my eyes were healed when I unselfishly gave up my hope of being able to see for the lives of others during the Iraq war. I have never felt that deep a degree of heartfelt willingness to give up something this big, especially something as important to me as my vision. Yet, I truly intended to give up my desire to see for others, and I believe it was at that moment that the miracle that was prayed for me was out there somewhere, just waiting for me to be pure enough to receive it. There is no other understanding or explanation for the sudden healing of my vision. With heartfelt sincerity, I prayed, "Thank you, God, for my vision," every night for many years, but as life went on and time passed, I forgot to give God thanks nightly, and how years later, in this busy world we call life, I sometimes even forget about my miracle.

I have come to realize that in this earthly world, it is hard to hold onto miracles. With the focus on daily living, children, and the challenges that accompany family life, work, friends, and stress, I couldn't hold my miracle securely in my mind. Life moved by so quickly, and to keep up with it, I had to be on the move as well. I would forget my miracle, and later, when I recalled it, I was ashamed that I'd forgotten about it. I pondered and wondered about Abbot David's words, how my "life would never be the same," though I hadn't perceived any change yet, with the very big exception that my physical sight had been restored.

CHAPTER 2

Diane

SUMMER 1990

Later in 1990, I felt sick at heart. It had been nearly two years since we'd moved from Sioux Falls, South Dakota, to Brookings, South Dakota, a small town in the Midwest, about an hour north of Sioux Falls. I was lonely, as I'd left my friends in Sioux Falls when we moved, and I had tried to keep up with them, but it was different now. I wasn't there with them any longer. I had not found a best friend in Brookings. I attended every social function the community had to offer. I met many nice people, but I had never felt that emotional "click," which to me felt like a best friend. Someone to share with and to support one another through life's ups and downs.

One morning, while traveling west on Third Street to my job at the Community Mental Health and Chemical Dependency Center, I passed a little blue Mazda that was traveling east. What I heard in that second that we passed one another was a man's voice saying, "There is your best friend." I was frantic! Where did that voice come from? I'd never heard a voice in my head before, and it shook me up. I wondered if I was crazy. What was also amazing was that I had a very clear look at this woman's face the second we drove by one another. I don't typically look at others when I drive for fear I'll drive off the road. The woman's face was friendly, warm, and inviting. She had big, blue eyes and a nice smile. As I looked in my rear-view mirror, I could see her car traveling east, farther away from me. How was I going to find this woman, and how was I going to tell her she was going to be my new best friend? I didn't want to sound like a lunatic, but this was indeed serious business! God, Jesus, or the Holy Spirit had never talked to me before!

Months passed, and I never saw her again. Yet, I believed I had heard the voice of God telling me she would become my best friend; I became discouraged and exhausted. I attended so many community functions and met so many nice folks, only to come up with another evening out, and I still had not met this woman.

One day, as I was dropping my four-year-old off at daycare, the director of the center stopped me as I was about to leave and asked me if I wanted to join her at Altrusa that day for lunch. She explained Altrusa was a group of professional working women, and I just might find it interesting. I was tired of meeting people, but reluctantly accepted her invitation to meet her at noon in one of the rooms at the Holiday Inn, where a buffet would also be served before a short program.

When I entered the room, I was met with a large group of women milling about. Some had already helped themselves to the buffet, while others were still standing and talking. As I looked around at all the people who already knew one another, I felt like an outsider. Suddenly, I saw the woman with a warm, friendly, and inviting face sitting at one of the tables with some other women. "Oh, my goodness!" I thought to myself, excited, but I felt I needed to look as if I was calm, while in my mind, I was doing a happy dance! There she was, my soon-to-be best friend! I continued to act in a professional, calm, "I have it all together" sort of manner. I tried not to jump up and down, saying, "Here you are, you are found!" I wondered how I would find a way to get to know her. "Hi, you're going to be my new best friend. You just don't know it yet." As it turned out, when I walked into the room, she later told me that she had turned to her friend and said, "Now there's a gal that looks like a lot of fun. I think we should get to know her." Later, she introduced herself and asked me if I liked flowers. "Yes, I love flowers!" I replied. That day, Diane invited me to her house for a light supper, where I also met several other people with whom I felt the "CLICK." Her backyard was like a bouquet of flowers, and it was a wonderful evening, just what my heart, soul, and social life had been lacking.

There was a sense of trust with Diane. She was easy to talk to, and we found ourselves confiding in one another not too long afterward. We took day trips in the car together, along with Mary and other friends. We three friends went on many fun and fabulous shopping trips to Minneapolis, Minnesota, a four-hour drive to the east, and Omaha, Nebraska, a four-hour drive to the south. We also attended several Broadway shows, which we loved. Diane owned a second home in Fort Myers, Florida. Diane invited Mary and me to come down for a week or two. We three friends would delight in the ocean and lie on the beach every day for a week or two every winter for years. Diane was a Christian as well, and she came to my aid more than a dozen times when I struggled with depression and anxiety. She accompanied me on errands when I was too anxious to go alone or too anxious to drive. She had sat in my car while I cried about the difficulties in my marriage or the depression that held me down. She saved me from my thoughts of hurting myself just by being there to listen. My depression had grown so severe that I actually thought my kids would be better off without me contaminating them with my mood disorder. At home, I lived in an old green bathrobe. Even one of my daughter's friends asked, "Why is your mother always in that green robe?" If I wasn't curled up on the couch with my mind in slumber, I was at work focusing on being a therapist for those who were depressed with marital problems, and numerous other issues, while I put myself aside and faked my joy. One thing that my depression and anxiety gave me was the ability to clearly identify, diagnose, and make recommendations to those dealing with depression and anxiety. However, I longed for the actual feeling of joy. I'd felt it before, and I wanted my life back. This was also a time when I sought out psychiatric medicine, which proved to give me periods of feeling less depressed. However, when I look back, Diane was a friend like no other. She was my therapist and a true-blue friend through thick and thicker. I am delighted to say I hold her friendship in my heart. It has been a treasured friendship and a gift to my life when I was in great need of a confidential and dear friend. I know it is true; Diane was a gift from God.

———————————

"Jesus said, 'This is my commandment, that you love one another as I have loved you. Greater love has no one than this, than to lay down one's life for his friends.'"

John 15:12-13, NKJV

THOUGHTS

Friendships, like marriages, are relationships of openness. When we are open and honest with one another, we cultivate true friendship. As we share with each other, we become emotionally intimate with one another. Jesus loves us and was open about his feelings for his disciples and His teachings from his heavenly father, God, with his disciples. Friendships are about loving others, and in my opinion, no one shows this better than Jesus to His disciples when He died on the cross for them. What did Jesus do? He laid down his life for his friends and all his future children like you and me. I believe there is no greater love than this. We also love our families. What parent wouldn't give up his/her life for their child to live? Just as Jesus gave up his life for us, His children.

CHAPTER 3

Nemo

FALL OF 1995

I was with her the evening she died. Nemo, my grandma, had told us for the past two days, "Jesus is coming, Jesus is coming!" She had been in a coma and had made this statement softly from her prone position in bed. However, today, as Dad and I sat in her room quietly talking to one another, her small, frail body suddenly bolted upright, and with a loud urgency in her voice, she raised both arms towards the ceiling and proclaimed, "Jesus is coming tomorrow!" Then, she lay back down as quickly as she had bolted upright, still in a coma. Dad and I looked at one another wide-eyed, saying nothing. I wondered, "Could she know?" I had read stories of these occurrences, and I wondered if we were witnessing one firsthand. I believed she knew, and there was no way I was going to miss tomorrow. When tomorrow came, I didn't want to go. I knew she would be leaving me, and I was grieving. I moved slowly through the day. I tried to avoid the inevitable. I didn't want her to die; I wanted her to stay in this world with me, but as the day unfolded, I felt a sudden urgency to get to her bedside. I drove the 90 miles between us quickly. I felt confused. Jesus was coming, and I wanted to be there when He arrived, but I didn't want to lose my grandma, "Nemo."

Nemo was 94 years old, and her body was giving out. She lived in a nursing home a year after her husband, my grandfather, had died. She saw me through childhood to adulthood. She was not only my grandma, but she was also my friend, and I was not only her granddaughter, but I was also her daughter. Nemo had one son, my father. I was her first grandchild and unable to pronounce the name "Mineva," and "Nemo" had come out instead. My parents, brothers, grandpa, her friends, and even her pastor called her "Nemo." The name had stuck! Nemo and I talked often, and she would call me when she was upset with Grandpa or when she was worried about my parents' marriage. I always listened to her concerns and tried to reassure her about things she could do nothing about. "Are you happily married?" she asked me. "Yes," I lied. Nemo had been restless earlier that evening, trying to speak words I struggled unsuccessfully to understand. She had been fretful and agitated despite my attempts to soothe her, and it broke my heart that I was unable to understand her, so I was relieved when the nurse came to check on her. Together, we wrapped her in another blanket to keep her warm and secure. Then the nurse quietly spoke to her, giving her permission to "let go whenever she was ready." I was stunned and angry to hear the nurse give her permission to die; who did the nurse think she was anyway, telling my grandma she could die whenever she was ready!? I remained beside Nemo's bed. I did not want her to die, so as the nurse spoke to her, I secretly stated the opposite of the nurse's words in my mind, believing Nemo would hear me and listen to me instead of the nurse. "No, don't go, don't listen to her, please don't leave me, I'm not ready yet, it's too soon, the nurse doesn't know what she's talking about, she's not family, and I'm too young to lose my grandma." As soon as I heard myself say those last few words, I realized the selfishness of my thinking, for I knew I had been very fortunate to still have my grandma at age forty-one when so many of my friends did not.

When the nurse left, I, too, began to say the words I knew Nemo needed to hear from family; I was grateful to have come to this awakening. Softly and slowly, I told Nemo it was okay to let go if she was ready to go to God. I told her she had lived a good and faithful life and that I believed Grandpa, her parents, and her baby brother were all waiting to be with her again. Her eyes opened then, and she watched me with intense stillness as I spoke. I held her hand, and I felt the pressure of her hand holding my hand back. I stroked her soft white hair, and I caressed her sweet face as she listened; she never spoke, the agitation gone. I told her we would all be fine, that we would go on to live good lives, and I thanked her for all the love she had given me. I could see she was at peace. As I talked with her, my tears fell across her face, neck, and chest. I wiped them off, laughing and crying as I said I was making a mess of her before she was going to meet the King! "Was that a hint of a smile on her lips?" I wondered. I was humming one of her favorite hymns, "Abide With Me," by Henry Francis Lyte, and then she closed her eyes to rest. The beautiful words echoed in my mind as I sat beside her.

"Abide with me: fast falls the eventide;
the darkness deepens; Lord, with me abide.
When other helpers fail and comforts flee,
Help of the helpless, O abide with me."

I had moved a chair alongside her bed, and for the first time, I realized how exhausted I was. I had an ache in my back from hours of sitting twisted on the edge of her bed, and as I stretched, I noticed a book on her bedside table titled "Where Angels Walk" by Joan Wester Anderson. This book is a series of stories compiled by the author.

I picked the book up, amused as Nemo's last name was Anderson. I settled down in the chair beside her to read. I held her hand under the covers; she was warm. I looked at my watch; it was 11:30 pm. I took a deep breath before I began to read and recalled Nemo's proclamation yesterday. I thought to myself, "Jesus, you have half an hour."

I was reading a story titled "Angel in the Cockpit." This particular story was about a pilot and his friend who were flying from Texas to North Carolina. Toward the end of their trip, they encountered unexpected fog, making it impossible for them to see, and the pilot radioed the air traffic controller in Asheville, requesting an emergency landing. The controller informed the pilot that their airport had been shut down due to the density of the fog and instructed them to return to Greenville to land. Frantic, the pilot informed the controller they didn't have enough fuel to return to Greenville, but no response came in return. They had lost connection with the controller. Flying blindly and fearing for their lives, they suddenly heard the controller come back online and began to direct them in for a visibly blind but safe landing. Once on the ground, the pilot thanked the controller for saving their lives. The controller's response caused both men to pause as he informed them they had lost all radio contact after he'd instructed them to return to Greenville. The pilot then knew it was God who had spoken directly to him, giving him instructions for a safe landing and saving their lives.

Before I could finish this short story, I became aware of a sense of peace that slowly began to fill me and eventually consumed me. I breathed in deeply and slowly as I sat relaxed in this blissful state of being. I felt comforted and peaceful, as though I had been resting for hours. There were none of the usual aches and pains, no tightness in my shoulders where I held my stress. When I opened my eyes, I saw ocean waves slowly filling Nemo's room, and as the waves became deeper, they leisurely ebbed and peaked from one wall to the other and back again. The waves were clear; I could see through them. Her room was overflowing with an ocean of peaceful stillness. The waves filled her room to the ceiling, then moved out the door and down the hallway. I wasn't startled when I realized I wasn't drowning, and I wasn't aware of feeling anything except exquisite peace and contentment. Calmly, I watched all this occur. I looked over my left shoulder to see if anyone had noticed the ocean of peace piling up in the hallway. I wondered how I was going to explain all this when I heard someone walking down the hall towards Nemo's room. As I turned to watch, the nurse walked right through the gigantic waves of peace! She didn't stumble or fall; she walked right through it, never noticing it at all! I couldn't believe she hadn't seen or felt it! I closed my eyes again and returned to this holy stillness. Time was different; it seemed too slow, or maybe it didn't exist at all. I felt fully rested and profoundly loved as I sat cradled within this sacred space.

The peace I felt was the only thing that mattered, the only thing I desired. I needed nothing, I wanted nothing, and I thought of no one, not even those most precious to me. I was within something luminous, something that buoyed me up and engulfed me in bliss. I was aware that every cell of my body was heightened with awareness, yet fully relaxed, joyfully content, and loved in some way that was beyond my human understanding.

The nurse touched my shoulder, and I became very aware of my bladder. It had been hours since I'd gone to the bathroom, and I absolutely had to go that very second. I couldn't believe I had not noticed my full bladder before. I asked the nurse to watch over Nemo, and before I dashed into her bathroom, I checked her. She looked serene and lovely. I noticed the peaceful ease in her beautiful face. I was gone only seconds, but when I returned, the nurse gently pointed out the blueness around Nemo's lips. The nurse started to listen to her heart through the stethoscope. I stood motionless as the minutes passed. The nurse listened. I watched Nemo, I watched the nurse, the nurse watched the clock, I watched the clock, minutes passed, and there were no more breaths. It was shortly before midnight, October twenty-first, nineteen ninety-five, when my grandmother, Mineva Anderson, physically died to this world and returned home to the Lord.

Once again, I picked up the phone to call my father, whom I had been unable to reach for hours. Sitting alongside Nemo's bed, I wept. I lay my head on her chest, seeking her comfort, and a short blast of air hit my face and shocked me. "Maybe she wasn't really dead," I thought. I searched her face and realized it had only been her final breath exiting her lungs under the weight of my head. I caressed her face and her white hair. I clung to the warmth of her skin under my touch. I kept hold of her hand and spoke softly to her. I knew she was with me because I felt her presence, but it was a very different presence now. I felt as if I was being comforted by her; it felt as if she were around my shoulders, hugging me.

When Dad came, we sat with her as we planned her funeral. It seemed the three of us talked it over together: her favorite hymns, who would sing, who would be pallbearers. We planned it all, the three of us. When the time came to call the funeral home, I told the funeral director not to hurry because Dad and I still wanted a little more time with her. When the funeral director arrived, it felt too soon. Dad and I helped him carefully lift Nemo's body onto the cot, and I positioned her head gently and supported it in the head-rest that was placed under her neck. We began to carefully wrap the body bag around her small frame. Tears rolled from Dad's eyes as he patted his mother's cheek, telling her she had been a good mama; he kissed her face, then hesitated a bit at her side before he moved to her feet and started to zip up the bag. I kissed her cheek one last time and lingered, noting the still warmth of her skin as I knew the next time I would see her, she would be embalmed. Her now soft, warm body would be hard and cold as stone. I slowly finished zipping the bag over her, watching her peaceful face disappear beneath its cover. I knew Nemo was no longer part of that body, that pale, sweet, small shell that housed her soul for ninety-four years. I felt her all around me, over my shoulder, above and behind now. Watching, comforting, and giving me strength as I had given her lifeless body my love, care, and kiss one last time.

By the time Dad and I left the nursing home, I was consumed by grief. It was about 1:30 AM. I drove thirty miles to my mother's house. I had wrapped myself in Nemo's shawl, crying, as I drove too fast through what seemed like endless darkness, yet feeling Nemo's presence with me all the way. When I arrived at Mom's, she opened the door, and her arms enveloped me as I entered her house. We sat, half talking, half crying as I tried to convey what I had experienced at Nemo's bedside and the peace that had filled me in her room when she died. I cried in frustration as I could not begin to communicate in human words the magnitude of the peace and love I had felt when Nemo died. Mom lovingly listened and nodded, quietly telling me it was a gift from God as she led my exhausted body up the stairs and tucked me into her guest bedroom. I remained wrapped in my grandma's shawl. I don't recall falling asleep, though I remember Mom's hand stroking my cheek as I cried, and I think she was murmuring a prayer, then morning came.

The following two years after Nemo went home to Jesus were very difficult for me. I slipped into a deep depression as I sought the peace I'd experienced at Nemo's bedside. My life felt empty in comparison to the peace and contentment I'd felt at her passing, and I cried myself to sleep each night wrapped in Nemo's shawl. I wanted to die. I begged God to let me die and come home to Him. I pleaded with God to allow me to return to His presence, to His peace, offering up my life for anyone in the world who was sick and didn't want to die. Yet, each morning, I woke up crying and feeling disillusioned. "How was I going to live in this earthly world after such a Heavenly experience that I had?" I clung to Nemo's shawl, seeking a fragment of comfort from this linking object to her. Nightly, I prayed to Nemo's spirit and to her angel and to my angel and to God. Through my angel, I sent her spirit messages each night, "I miss you so much, I don't know how to go on living anymore." I felt anger and hopelessly betrayed by a God who gave me a brief taste of the world beyond and the unbelievable "peace that passes all understanding" and then left, abandoning me to this earth to live with all the mundane and unimportant things that are of such great significance to human beings. I wondered, where do people who have had these divine experiences like this belong? How do they survive living on this earth? I felt I didn't belong on this earth anymore.

Two years and two months later, the night before Christmas, I had a dream.

I dreamt I entered my home, and as I looked up into my kitchen from where I stood in the foyer, there was Nemo. She stood with her back leaning against my kitchen counter. Even though my mother was still alive, in my dream, Mom stood at Nemo's side. The kitchen was full of bodies that moved about, and I recall they were family, yet I didn't see anyone's face. I only saw Nemo. From where I stood, stunned and unable to move, I watched as she began to smile at me. She was beaming a heavenly light from her heart. She looked wonderful, younger, rested, and well. Her blue eyes sparkled as she stretched out her arms to me. I ran up the steps and into her arms. I held her tightly, crying with joy. I told her I was so happy to see her again! Then abruptly, I stepped back, gripping her arms and searching her face as I implored her to tell me, "How could this be? You have been dead," I said. "I know because I was with you." Both faces spoke the truth as life eternally shone from within their bodies. Nemo beamed. Mom nodded assuredly, "Yes, it is true!" Then I woke up. I felt something wasn't right. I felt bewildered and skeptical as I began to realize I had been dreaming. I was sure I'd been awake and that what I had just experienced was real, not that I'd been sleeping and had just woken from a dream. It didn't feel or seem like a dream; it felt completely real and powerful to me.

Christmas morning at Mom's house, my brother said they had a "Christmas present for me from Nemo." Shocked by his words, I scolded him for joking like that. Then he said he was serious, that they had recently found a gift wrapped and addressed to me in their laundry room behind the dryer. He thought it must have fallen back there two Christmases ago when Nemo was with us at their house. I began to cry, overwhelmed by the dream I'd just had the night prior and now this physical gift from Nemo. I knew this was no coincidence; this was providence in action. A gift from Nemo to remind me of the gift of her life. I was learning the promises of God's gift of life and fidelity to me and to all of us.

I believe Nemo's spirit came to me in a dream to reassure me that she was joyful and alive. I felt these words were inadequate human words to describe a heavenly experience. In that very instant, my grieving of Nemo changed; I felt a physical lift in my heart. I believe I was released from the grip of my bereavement. I still longed for her and deeply missed her, yet my grief was transformed. I was able to let her go. I had seen it in my dream, the truth and confidence in her and Mom's faces as Divine radiance shone from within them. I had questioned, "How could you be here as you are dead?" But no, my faith was understanding that Nemo's soul was not dead but that it had risen. She was still here. She was everywhere, as was God, and as it is with God's people.

Nemo's death was a magnificent one, as is life eternal!

"For God so loved the world that he gave his one and only Son, that whoever believes in him shall not perish but have eternal life"

John 3:16

"Don't let your hearts be troubled. Trust in God, and trust also in me. There is more than enough room in my Father's home. If this were not so, would I have told you that I am going to prepare a place for you? When everything is ready, I will come and get you, so that you will always be with me where I am."

John 14:1-3, NLT

"The ecstasy is beyond human word, God's ecstatic love for all His children. As that spiritual experience came to an end with Nemo's physical death, a single thought was placed in my mind: God's call to all his children, 'Love one another as I have loved you.'"

John 13:34

THOUGHTS

I think this experience was given to me because I've felt alone for most of my life and more so since Nemo's death, but I now understand that there is something in this universe that is beyond my physical self, something bigger than I can believe in and count on. It is more powerful than anything I have experienced before. I know God gave me a brief glimpse of life beyond this human one. I believe the magnitude of the peace and the power of that holy stillness that I felt was the presence of Jesus. And as Nemo passed from my hand to God's hand, I was allowed to feel a sliver of the living God. I believe God's love for his children is far too great for human consumption. I have no doubt this is true; I just don't know why, as it was extremely difficult to go on living afterward. I now understand that I am never alone if Jesus is in my life, and my life has become all the richer for it. My human desire to follow the power of that perfect peace and Divine love into forever was far too great for me to handle. My single focus was to follow that Divine love I experienced at Nemo's bedside. I was not thinking about my life on earth or leaving my family and friends. I didn't even think of my most beloved dear children. I simply did not want to be separated from that Divine love! Perhaps what we call death on earth is actually birth into heaven. My experience tells me that it would be impossible for anyone to experience the depth of God's love for all His children. I believe our human bodies would explode as we, here on earth, are not woven together in a way to contain God's great love for us. That is saved for a heavenly experience when we go home to God.

Nemo had proclaimed, "Jesus is coming tomorrow!" He did for her, and He does today and every day for each one of us.

CHAPTER 4

Coffee and God?

FALL OF 1997

There I was, in the bathroom of a popular coffee shop, hiding out from God. I tried to buy time; I put my head in my hands. My hands were shaking, and I felt beads of sweat gathering along my hairline. My heart was racing. I whispered, "Okay, God, is this YOU talking to me?" I didn't want anyone outside the bathroom door to hear me because this incident reminded me of lunacy and auditory hallucinations. But there I was, sitting on the toilet, nervously listening as no God thoughts, no words of instruction, no complete sentences popped uninvited into my mind. I looked around the bathroom; hair and dirt were on the floor. I pulled up the legs of my jeans so they did not touch the floor. "Ugh, germs, I hate public bathrooms," I thought to myself as I sat waiting. "Waiting for what?" I asked myself, and I started to feel more confident as all was silent.

My dear friend Diane and I were leaving Minneapolis, Minnesota, where we'd had a girls weekend away. We stopped at a coffee shop before starting the four-hour drive home. Diane got in line to place her coffee order while I picked up juice, paid, and sat down at the first available table. The tables were incredibly small—I wondered how anyone could be expected to eat off them. They were spaced so closely together that I was instantly aware of the couple at the table to my left. They sat with heads together in deep conversation.

"I practice my music daily, hoping it will be good enough one day to share with others," the woman said. "Your musical talents are wonderful," the man reassured her. His head was pulled in towards her as he spoke more quietly. I tried not to listen, but the tables were too close for a private conversation to remain private. "Sometimes it's hard for me to leave the house, and pretending everything is fine is becoming more difficult. I feel depressed, anxious, exhausted, and unhappy. I want to be honest about my feelings, but I'm afraid of being misunderstood and rejected by others, even my spouse," the woman said.

The man looked at the woman with kind eyes and spoke to her with a gentle voice. He seemed attentive to her feelings. The woman gripped her napkin in both hands and twisted it back and forth, and small, shredded bits of napkin were strewn on the table between them, but she didn't seem to notice. I sipped my juice, trying to mind my own business even though I was not successful in that endeavor.

I am a counselor and a Christian, and I believed I was called to be kind towards others; however, hearing this woman's personal sharing was beginning to annoy me! I didn't want to hear about anyone else's personal troubles. It was like hearing my own problems and those of my clients. In my mind, I began to assess and diagnose this woman: *Major Depression, single episode, moderate, without psychotic features, diagnostic code 296.23 and Anxiety Disorder with Panic Attacks, rule out Agoraphobia, diagnostic code 300.01. (Diagnostic Criteria from the DSM IV that was used at that time).* I wondered if anyone had told this poor woman there are medications for this problem. "What's wrong with me?" I wondered to God, then I remembered, "This is what I do for a living!"

Tell her. I raised my eyebrows as I shrugged off the thought. After a few seconds, the voice comes again. *Tell her.* This completely formed message had just appeared in my mind, and yet it seemed not to be my own thought at all. I was feeling confused and wondered where this voice, or thought, had come from. "What was it exactly—a voice or a thought?" I pondered. "Had I thought a thought and not been aware of my own thinking?" I was worried.

"What the heck," I silently asked back.

"Tell her what?" I asked.

Tell her. The voice came again. I felt nervous, but I smiled, which is what I do to deflect anxiety while trying to lighten up. I consider the possibility that this is not a coffee shop at all but a set for *The Twilight Zone.* I chuckle, thinking I was funny.

Diane joins me at the table. I tried to whisper to her what was going on inside my head. I waved her closer with my right hand, trying to get her to move her head closer to mine; I didn't want to be overheard. My breath was getting caught on my words, and my left hand was shaking under the table where I held it tightly between my crossed legs.

Once again, the voice interrupted, *Tell her.*

I wanted to yell, "Tell her what?" but who would I be yelling at?

The voice said, *"Tell her to be strong and brave. Tell her to follow her heart, and she is a good and genuine person. Tell her she will be alright,"* the voice said.

"No," my thoughts instinctively barked back. "She will think I'm rude; this is none of my business. Leave me alone. He is her friend; he is supportive of her. I needed to mind my own business and stay out of it."

I was near tears and felt helpless as I silently pleaded my case. I began to wonder what was wrong with me, and the assessment and diagnosis started against me. "Yes, I'm going to have to start diagnosing myself seriously, according to the *Diagnostic and Statistical Manual of Mental Disorders IV (DSM IV),* because I am now experiencing auditory hallucinations!"

I caught Diane looking at me with a "What's up?" kind of expression as I wondered, "Is this God speaking to me? Is God nudging me?" I dismissed the idea, knowing I was not special enough for God to speak to me, and I felt panicky and sweaty as I excused myself to hide in the bathroom.

Now, there I was, sitting on the toilet seat in still silence. Suddenly, I felt a force pushing my body forward, like a tornado spinning against my back. It was clear there were no more negotiations. It was absolute. Yes, this was God talking to me, and I must do as instructed! I was perspiring, my hands cold and clammy, and my heart was racing wildly. This was a coffee shop restroom, for heaven's sake—not a mountain top or a burning bush. Gosh, I'm funny, I thought. But I was propelled to talk to the woman, so I frantically jumped off the toilet and quickly opened the bathroom door. I sighed in relief to see the couple still sitting at the small table. Fearing they might have already left and I would not be able to fulfill what I'd been told to say, gave me an awful feeling of dread. Then I saw Diane waiting for me at the exit door. With one thought in mind, I walk over to Diane and say, "Wait a minute, there's something I have to do."

I approached the couple's table. I felt dreadfully nervous, and my hands were shaking. I wondered how I was going to say this. I gently touched the woman's arm, and I heard myself say, "I felt compelled by God to tell you that you are a brave and strong woman, that you are a good and genuine person, and that you must be true to yourself, and you will find your way. I am so sorry for interrupting you. I wasn't trying to eavesdrop on your conversation, and I don't mean to be rude, but I have this compelling feeling that I couldn't leave here without telling you this." The man's mouth dropped open and turned into a kind smile as he stood, extending his hand. The woman remained seated. Her eyes widened as she sat speechless. The man introduced himself as a Minister of Music at their church, and the woman introduced herself and told me her name. She thanked me for what I had just told her. I began to babble about how embarrassed I had felt, and then I abruptly stopped and said, "Goodbye, I need to go home now," as I all but ran out of the coffee shop.

Once in the safety of Diane's vehicle, she turned to me with a puzzled look and asked, "What was that all about?" I explained to her the voices in my head, the conversations, someone speaking to me, and my answering. I was talking a mile a minute and asking her if she thought I was crazy because I was feeling very crazy.

"What just happened to me?" I implored her for a plausible answer when suddenly I heard the flapping of wings, and they began to flap louder and louder until I could hear nothing else. I hollered at Diane, "Do you hear those wings flapping?" Her eyebrows bunched together as she shook her head, "No." Suddenly, tears of immense joy began to spill from my eyes. I hadn't felt like crying, but there I was, bawling my eyes out because of the fantastic joy I was feeling. I believed the flapping wings were either an angel or the Holy Spirit, God's way of gifting me for my act of obedience in saying what He told me to say to the woman. I finally understood God wanted me to tell the woman in the coffee shop what He told me to tell her, and once I'd been a faithful daughter of the King, I believe He blessed me with His goodness. God was with me; this was Him at work. I felt overjoyed. As suddenly as my tears of joy began, they abruptly stopped! I looked at Diane, void of tears yet filled with the most magnificent peacefulness beyond my human understanding.

"For the word of God is living and active, sharper than any two-edged sword, piercing to the division of soul and of spirit, of joints and of marrow, and discerning the thoughts and intentions of the heart."

Hebrews 4:12, ESV

"Do not merely listen to the word...Do what it says."

James 1:22

"But be doers of the word, and not hearers only, deceiving yourselves. For if anyone is a hearer of the word and not a doer, he is like a man observing his natural face in a mirror; for he observes himself, goes away, and immediately forgets what kind of man he was. But he who looks into the perfect law of liberty and continues *in it*, and is not a forgetful hearer but a doer of the work, this one will be blessed in what he does."

James 1:22-25, NKJV

THOUGHTS

This was a bizarre situation for sure, but a powerful one for me. I recall how much I did not want to interrupt the couple talking. Yet the panic I'd felt after I'd been pushed out of the bathroom, fearing the couple had left the coffee shop and I wouldn't be able to accomplish what I'd been instructed to do, also felt like a devastating outcome. I think it's important to reiterate that only good comes from God/Jesus/and the Holy Spirit. Hearing an auditory voice is not a normal thing in my profession. It's often a time to encourage a client to seek inpatient treatment for their own safety. This is where it's necessary to look for the fruit of the Spirit. Is it good fruit or bad fruit, according to the outcome? For nothing bad or evil comes from God/Jesus/the Holy Spirit: only goodness and purity comes from God/Jesus/the Holy Spirit. If a person tells you that God told them to hurt someone. That is evil and the work of the evil one.

If we, as God's people, prepare ourselves by reading God's Holy word, trying to understand the meaning of what we read in the Bible, join a Bible study group, attend church, or make quiet time on a regular basis to pray, then we may hear God's voice or feel God's nudges, or hear God in our thoughts. We may think about helping another or doing something kind for someone with no personal gain. That is the goodness of God inside you. Only goodness and Christian love comes from God. I believe after I'd been a faithful servant of the Lord and told the woman what God told me to tell her, I was gifted with hearing those powerful angel wings, or perhaps they were the wings of the Holy Spirit. Those wings flapped so loudly I could hear nothing else, and the joy that poured through me were blessed tears from my eyes. It is the only answer that makes any sense to me regarding an experience that made no sense at all! I catch myself here, as we humans are always trying to make sense out of everything, and sometimes that simply does not work. Psychiatrist Fritz Perls coined a phrase in Gestalt Therapy that said, "Lose your mind and come to your senses!" To focus on the present moment is the goal of Gestalt Therapy.

CHAPTER 5

The Poem God Wrote

SUMMER 2000

In the summer of 2000, I attended the School for Spiritual Direction, the same school my mother attended in Pecos, New Mexico, when my eyes were healed by God, which was now offered in San Miguel, California. Once again, it would be led by Abbot David Geraets from the Monastery of the Risen Christ, San Luis Obispo, California. Abbot David and I had been corresponding since the healing of my vision, and I had asked him to pray for the future of my marriage. It was his suggestion that I come to the school for spiritual direction.

When the time came, Mom and my friends gathered around me at the airport and prayed that I would find the courage I needed for the answers I sought. This was before 9/11, when people could accompany the passenger up to the gate. Mom and my friends were aware of the difficulties in my marriage, my depression, and my anxiety of living in a loveless marriage, as they often sat with me in my car while I cried.

The two weeks at the School for Spiritual Direction were filled with classes taught by Abbot David, my spiritual director, Dr. Marie, a Ph.D. psychologist and Benedictine Oblate, Catholic priests, and brothers trained in various areas of specialty such as religion, spirituality, Jung's depth psychology, art, and journaling dreams, and dream interpretation. All the lectures were wonderful, but what I loved the most was listening to Abbot David's teachings. I felt like a little child sitting at the feet of Jesus when Abbot David spoke of his knowledge of the Bible and experiences with God, Jesus, and the Holy Spirit. I knew I was in the presence of a holy man; I could feel it, and I already felt a special closeness to Abbot David due to his prayers for the healing of my vision years earlier. Dr. Marie's insights into my marriage, my fears of divorce, my personality as a caregiver, my dreams, values, and my misplaced sacrifices were shocking and amazingly helpful to me.

One day in group therapy, Dr. Marie said to me, "Kristin, Jesus already died on the cross for you, so why do you continue to sacrifice yourself in this marriage?" This question caught me off guard and gave me much to think about with respect to my constant attempts to save my marriage, as I had believed a faithful wife would do, with the vows that I made before God. My dread of divorce and how I had been hanging on to my marriage, unhealthy as it was, sacrificing my mental health and my self-worth while crying out to God in prayer to help fix it, over and over and over. It was the first time I considered that perhaps it was not God's will to fix my marriage.

I also participated in a small group, which was scary and very risk-taking for me. I've never been a "group" person, and as a counselor, I'd always had the comfort of being the facilitator of groups, not a participant. Despite my nervousness, I became a part of a group of compassionate people who eventually felt amazingly safe for me to open up to. One of the few times that I prayed aloud, something I never did because of my low feelings of self-confidence, one of our group members began speaking in tongues as I prayed over her. This was an amazing experience for both of us. It was something she'd never experienced but wanted to be able to do, and something I never considered happening, but it caused me to think that maybe I had a connection with God after all.

Also, classes were offered on spiritual growth, physical wellness, music therapy, prayer time, the Enneagram, journaling dreams, and dream interpretation. We also walked the Labyrinth, experienced healing services, poetry, quiet time, morning praise, the Eucharist, and evening vespers. We washed one another's feet, as Jesus did. When Abbot David washed my feet, I trembled, for this was a holy man who washed my dusty feet. In turn, I washed his feet, which gave me a sense of deep humility. Our meals were eaten together, and for two weeks during the summers of 2000 and 2001, I lived the life of a monk in the sweltering California desert, and I'd never felt happier.

The rooms were sparse. Mine contained twin beds, a battered bedside table, an old lamp, a small sink with running water, and one tiny mirror: evidently, monks don't care about how their hair looks. There was an outlet. There was a small kneeling altar which I immediately placed in the closet because I didn't believe I would be that vulnerable. There was a Bible and a hard, straight-backed chair.

The temperature in this part of the country can reach 115 degrees in the summertime, and the Mission had no air-conditioning. The cement block walls were deep and wide, which kept the building comfortable, and the windows were open all day, allowing the dry desert breezes to blow through. It was wonderful! What was good enough for the monks who dedicated their life's work to God through study, prayer, and work was good enough for me! The accommodation, though sparse, was surprisingly plentiful. I was happy and content. I had all I needed and so much more. I was surprised and discovered I didn't need a lot of stuff to live and feel happy. The lifestyle, daily routine, and structure of the Mission gave me a sense of internal structure, peace, and security I'd never felt before. I had begun to understand how one could spend one's life in service and in prayer with the Lord, as the peace and contentment I tasted were sustaining.

It was after the first summer session when I was back home and trying to keep the spiritual lessons I'd learned alive in my daily prayer and meditation, while I tried to live out what I'd learned by my words and actions, that this next spiritual experience occurred.

I had been in prayer, sitting on my bed and meditating within the feeling of peace, when suddenly a completely formed thought dropped into my mind. The thought instructed me, without words, to "get paper and a pen," and in doing this, I rushed back to sit on my bed, wondering what was going to happen next. I felt propelled to write, but I didn't know what I was supposed to write. I had nothing in mind, so I put the tip of the pen on the paper as if I were ready to write. Waiting, I felt transfixed yet completely unaware of where this was going. Suddenly, I began to write as fast as I could, trying to keep up as one word entered my mind, another word followed, and this continued intensely for what seemed about a minute. I also felt led to write it line for line, just as I have done below. The last three words of the poem were the only ones I can claim. I spoke those words spontaneously and aloud as an overwhelming expression of emotion after I had completed writing God's poem. It was perfect! God doesn't need any rewrites!

"I am black
My hair is long
Very long
Wild kinky free
Music moves me
Grooves me
Wailing, clappin' chantin' freedom songs.
My Father's blood runs through my veins.
I am woman.
I am man.
I am child.
Old, young, tall, short, large and small.
I am Red, Brown, Yellow, Black, and White
And shimmering Purple and Orange
For the forgotten ones.
I am sane, insane, homeless, rich, roaming,
Lost.
I am a hero.
I am all people.
But mostly
I am Black as night

And I sing light into the darkness of the human soul.
And I move gently across the waters
And the world lays its head
Upon my bosom"

"....... ah, sweet Jesus," I whisper.

"In the beginning of the Bible, it talks about the Holy Spirit hovering over the waters. In the beginning, 'God created the heavens and the earth. Now the earth was formless and empty, darkness was over the surface of the deep, and the Spirit of God was hovering over the waters.'"

Genesis 1:1-2

"In the last days, God says, I will pour out my Spirit on all people. Your sons and daughters will prophesy, your young men will see visions, your old men will dream dreams. Even on my servants, both men and women, I will pour out my Spirit in those days, and they will prophesy."

Acts 2:17-18

THOUGHTS

The vision that settled in my mind as this poem was being written was that of a Black woman with long, black, curly hair. Her hair extended from the beginning of time to eternity. The woman was connected to the sky and to the waters of the earth. She was bending horizontally over the world, checking on all her children. I felt she was connected to everything and that she felt whatever her children felt. All joys, all sorrows, and all devastations. I do not mean to imply that God is black or white, or any color. I believe God is Spirit form. I also believe that when Jesus returns, he will come as a man. I believe God is limitless and boundless in His ways of coming to His people. Nothing is impossible for God, and we are free to see Him in any way we need. God covers all.

CHAPTER 6

This Is the Year...

SPRING 2001

A man's voice states, "This is the year you will be divorced." From a sound sleep, I awoke hearing myself loudly yelling back, "No, I won't!" Then, sleepily, I sat up in bed and said aloud, "What?" "Hello," "Is somebody there?" as I crawled out of bed and searched the house, no one was home. Our two children were on sleepovers.

But where did that voice come from, and why would he say what he said? I wasn't going to get divorced; I still had my commitment to our marriage. Even though we were the Grand Canyon, with him on one side and me on the other side, with miles between us. I'd been holding myself together for years. I wasn't ready to give up now. I didn't want to be divorced, and I didn't want to be part of that group.

Still, who was talking to me?

God?

My depression and anxiety had begun to lift. But this is what my depression looked like:

THE CLIFF

"In my mind's eye, I reside under a cliff. The overhang is life above me. I knew the sun shone up there, though I couldn't see or feel it from my perch below the surface edge. I knew there were living, breathing human beings up there, but I did not care to see or be seen. I was content to remain under the overhang of the cliff, my refuge. I lie in the fetal position, satisfied within the secure ball of my body.

When I had to leave my shelter, I would feel afraid. I pondered it for hours in the early morning darkness. Dread filled me. When I could no longer put off rising, I flung myself up and over the steep and rocky edges of the cliff that lived within my soul. This exhausted me. I scraped my knees on the rocks and clung to the ground beneath me with my nails dug into the dirt. My position secured, I dropped one leg out of my bed, and the other leg followed. My limbs felt like weights. I plod my way to the bathroom and urinate for what seems an eternity. I am reminded I felt the need to urinate hours ago; my inability to muster the energy to get up forced me to hold it. I secretly marvel and praise myself for my high tolerance for discomfort and wonder why no one has ever applauded me for that.

Once in a vertical position, I attempt to greet my children with the love and warmth I feel for them, even though I look and feel like shit. I tell my children, "I'm just overtired. I'll feel better eventually." Surely, I had achieved hiding this feeling inside me. Surely, they would not notice or be too concerned. Would they recognize their 'super mom' was a wreck? I gazed downward at my disheveled self; mismatched socks, Birkenstocks, and my old green bathrobe surrounded and comforted me in a circle of warmth. I sank a bit farther into my spot in the perch within my couch.

The phone rang. I covered my head. I am not home. I am dead.

It was January 1st, 2001. It was a year like all the others, stormy. I had removed my wedding rings years prior and had replaced them with one of Nemo's gold bands. I was emotionally gone. I lived an emotionally separate life even though we shared the same home.

This part of my life, 26 years to be exact, would be one of the longest chapters in my spiritual memoir. While I feel the spiritual experiences given to me helped me live through some of the darkest, rawest times in my life, I have intentionally left our marital maladjustments out of this book. They will remain just between the two of us. I did this for my children, as they have requested this of me. With this in mind, I will only talk about myself and how I let our marriage down.

I am humbled to say that after twenty-four years of being divorced, we can be together for family gatherings and be friendly, kind, and thoughtful towards one another. In some ways, I shall always love him. This did not happen quickly for me, but over time and with a great deal of prayer. I have come to care for him again in a different way and want the best for him. Because of our children and all those we both love and care about, in some ways, we will always be family.

Later in the year, I recalled that male voice declaring, "This is the year you will be divorced," and I realized it had happened just as the voice said it would.

"Call to me and I will answer you and tell you great and unsearchable things you do not know."

Jeremiah 33:3

"Here I am! I stand at the door and knock. If anyone hears my voice and opens the door, I will come in to him and eat with him, and they with me."

Revelations 3:20

"Your word is a lamp for my feet, a light on my path."

Psalm 119:105

"Wives, submit yourselves to your husbands, as is fitting in the Lord. Husbands, love your wives and do not be harsh with them."

Colossians 3:18-19

THOUGHTS

In all the years we were married, it never dawned on me to turn to the Bible, where Paul talks about husbands loving their wives as Christ loved the church (Ephesians 5:25). I am ashamed to admit this, for as much as I was praying by asking God to bring us closer together, I was not in the image of the church; I was not holy or blameless. I was not saying words to build him up and help him in his strengths as a man. "A wife of noble character who can find? She is worth far more than rubies. Her husband has full confidence in her and lacks nothing of value. She brings him good, not harm, all the days of her life"

(Proverbs 31:10-12). (The teaching of kindness is on her tongue; the heart of her husband trusts in her.)

I was to be a helper, and I was not. I was critical and demanding; I was not understanding, nor did I let my spouse lean upon my shoulders at the end of a long, arduous day. I was engulfed by my own long day as a married, depressed, and single parent.

I don't want to end this portion with the reader thinking we never had good times, for we did. They were just sprinkled in and amongst the hard times. The good times never lasted very long, but when we had them, they were treasured. At times, I believed I could love this man forever, yet that was not the path taken.

I have some family, friends, and former clients who have had marriages where both spouses adore one another. It is a gift to my soul and an honor to have been in the presence of this kind of love. It seems that if a husband loves his wife as God loves the church, and a wife honors her husband, she would be so well-loved that she would hold nothing back in loving him. Both would be in symmetry to one another and to the nature of the word as it is written in the Bible. It is at this place in my life that I now take Jesus as my lover and partner in life. Although I wanted to be married "til death do us part," now I physically walk alone, but I am emotionally and spiritually stronger, and I understand I am never really alone with Jesus in my heart. The spiritual experiences He has blessed me with leave me with great comfort, far beyond human comfort, love, and far beyond my human understanding. I know I can turn to Him for anything in my life. I may not live in a monastery, but I devote the rest of my life to loving Jesus. My focus is now on loving my family and friends and prayerfully bringing peace and harmony to the world in Jesus' name.

CHAPTER 7

The Deaf Woman Hears

SEPTEMBER 2003

I remarried (more about this in chapter nine) in September of 2003. We went on a mission trip to the Dominican Republic for the second half of our honeymoon. The first half was a week in Maui.

Sitting comfortably in the van and as we drove through the Capital of the Dominican Republic, Santo Domingo, I watched as entire families clung to one another as they whizzed by on old mopeds. We saw a stripped-down moped with an old washing machine strapped behind the driver. The driver was wearing jeans and a dirty, sleeveless t-shirt, which blew against his body as he zipped by. Other vehicles carried people clutching chickens while weaving their way in and around the traffic, cramming every inch of the highway. Old vans and cars sped past us, allowing us to glimpse inside vehicles that had neither doors nor seats, yet held people who were packed full inside.

Elderly people with weathered faces and little children without shoes flocked to the center of the freeway, trying to peddle their beaded necklaces, bracelets, woven baskets, or paintings. I was afraid these people would be killed or maimed as cars sped wildly past them. Some of the older people rested on their haunches at the curbside while the younger ones took up the task of selling.

"How do these people live?" I wondered as I watched from the comforts of an air-conditioned van. Inside the van, people were talking in Spanish and English. We sat comfortably; we were not crowded. I could not clearly hear what was going on outside in the street; it sounded like a constant honking of horns in different tones as a frantic theme played out on the freeway, and drivers switched lanes without the use of blinkers.

We left the paved highway, taking narrow dirt roads up and down hills, around corners, through a never-ending sea of poverty. Little children waved to us as they ran naked down dirt roads. Many of the volunteers had been there before. Some recognized the children. I sat in shock. Small drug stores, shacks really, appeared along the corners of the dirt roads with signs in English advertising candy, pop, and beer, scribbled or spray-painted on the side of the shack, but there were no shoppers. Rubber tires, broken tire rims, broken furniture, broken bicycles, broken cars, broken pick-ups, broken bed frames, old mattresses, anything that was broken ended up here in the barrio. As we drove, I watched clouds of dust billow up behind our van and blow into shanty-like homes that had no windows or doors. It seemed like an entire nation of people. In fact, generations of families were born, lived, raised their families, and died inside this enormous overflow where everything was broken, worn out, and had been thrown away.

People with curious faces stuck their heads out of holes in walls as we passed. I wondered what they were thinking. Had they heard we were coming and were waving to welcome us, or was their wave a simple gesture of kindness to strangers who traveled by on their dusty roads? We had been told the Dominicans were a peaceful, friendly, loving people, but as I watched them watch us, I felt a prickly heat upon my skin. I was keenly aware I was a stranger in their land.

My new husband and I had joined a group of missionaries from The First Presbyterian Church in Winston-Salem, North Carolina. These volunteers had committed a week of their time, expertise, and donations of medical, dental, and construction materials for people needing homes and health care in one of the poorest areas of the Dominican Republic.

The Executive Director of Mission Emanuel was Jack Larson. I looked around the airport, wondering how we would recognize Jack. People were everywhere. I didn't know which way to go, so I followed the crowd through customs and out of the building to the top of a ramp, where I caught a glimpse of the man who I knew must be Jack. People were excited, talking and laughing as they enveloped this man with hugs, handshakes, smiles, and pats on the back. Jack emerged to greet those of us he did not know. He was a tan, middle-aged man wearing a t-shirt and a pair of blue jeans. He had brown hair, a big smile, a friendly face, and a round belly. He greeted me as if we were old friends, and instantly, I felt comfortable in his company.

Jack Larson, the Director of Mission Emmanuel, the Dominicans, and missionaries have built up a community of two schools, kindergarten through twelfth grade, a home for the principal and his family, old offices were set up for a medical clinic and a dental clinic, and past missionaries built a three-story church and a parsonage. Many concrete homes have been built for families in the communities of Nazareth and Cielo, two of the poorest areas near Santo Domingo, the Capital of the Dominican Republic. Jack was an unpretentious man, a true missionary who, through God's calling, has dedicated his life's work to Mission Emanuel. He was a selfless leader who, for the past half-century, has put his heart and soul into organizing groups of volunteers and missionaries to work alongside Dominicans to improve their way of life through spreading the Good News of Jesus Christ, providing health care, education, and better living conditions. For years, Jack worked tirelessly to recruit volunteer groups from the United States. Now the volunteers are on a waiting list to work with Jack.

For a student to attend school, the Dominican Law required they wear uniforms, which most Dominican families cannot afford. However, due to the hard work of compassionate Christians and others who sponsor children, over 400 students were able to attend school.

Most of the Dominicans' homes were constructed of corrugated cardboard or stripped pieces of tin assembled with wires or ropes for makeshift walls or roofs, which provided little protection from the blistering sun and torrential rains. I'd never seen poverty like this before. Some homes were built under groupings of trees, others into a hillside. When the rain came, the homes built into the hillside were quickly seized by flood waters, tons of mud that swept everything from the dirt floors of their homes to the bottom of the hill and into the brown, muddy gully below.

Having reached our first destination, we piled out of the van to stretch. This was the site where the medical and dental crew would set up their clinics to see patients for the next five days. I was told a multitude of people would be standing in line every day, all day long, in the blistering heat, waiting to see the doctor, nurses, and dentists.

Back in the van, the rest of us rode a short distance up the hill to unload the construction equipment. A few other women and I were a part of this construction group. The men quickly began to organize as they prepared to level the earth to build a concrete foundation. Being part of a team to build a home for a family was going to be exciting, I thought. Then I saw the children.

They stood barefoot on the curb across the gravel road. I waved, and they waved back, smiling. They had toothy grins and beautiful black eyes that sparkled with curiosity. Their dark hair was mostly curly, but some of the girls had woven beautiful and intricate braids into their hair. Some of the younger children wore old, worn-out underwear that barely hung on their little hips, elastic long gone. Some wore nothing at all, their clothes too large or too small for their young bodies. I learned that what they wore had been donated by former volunteers through the years. Their shoes went from no-name to brand names like Nike, Asics, and their plain, worn-out t-shirts from faded colors to Abercrombie and Fitch, juxtaposing American fashion and poverty.

The children's playground was the street where the boys played kickball, and the girls sat on the curb weaving one another's hair, but now they were drawn to the construction site. They wanted to watch us and ask questions about what we were building. However, for their own safety, the men in our group who spoke Spanish told them time and time again to stay on the other side of the road where it was safer, away from the ladders and nails that had fallen on the ground. Like a slight breeze, they somehow seemed to drift back into the middle of the construction area, barefoot and all. It was difficult for this curious little group to stay put, so when one of the men suggested I stay with them, I decided to walk them back to the other side of the road. I sat down with them on the concrete curb that ran along both sides of the dirt road. Little did I know, I was about to get the job I would have for the week. At first, the children and I just sat together in silence as we watched the building crew across the road. They tried to speak to me in Spanish, but I told them in English I didn't know any Spanish. "No Espanola," I said, holding up the palms of my hands and trying to look as if I were saying, "Sorry, but oh well." I tried to tell them I was from America, and they all nodded and muttered among themselves, saying, "Si, Americanas," as a few of them patted me on the back as if we were old friends. I tried to tell them I was with Jack's group. The kids again conferred with one another, nodding their heads in agreement, saying, "Si, Jack, mi amigo." Yes, Jack, he is my friend. After about ten minutes, I understood why the children were having trouble sitting along the concrete curb. It was sweltering hot, and my back was already starting to ache. I stretched out my legs across the water trickling down the gutter, feeling the discomfort of the concrete curb beneath me. The little children started jumping up and down barefoot in the water as it trickled down the curb. As I watched the children play, my legs and new tennis shoes got splattered.

Pointing to one child at a time, I asked in Spanish, "Hombre?" "What is your name?" They took turns telling me their names and asking mine, which they easily said over and over. Whether any of us understood one another during that week will remain a mystery, but soon, they spoke to me as if I were one of them. The girls whispered secrets in my ears, and the boys spoke fast, constantly telling me things and pointing in different directions. I kept reminding them I didn't speak Spanish, "No Espanola," I'd say as I put my hand over my heart to convey that I was sorry, but that didn't seem to matter to the children as we sat together on the curb. I listened, smiled, laughed, and teased them. They put their arms around my shoulders, and their little hands found their way into mine. I didn't understand what they had said, but I knew we had become friends. Despite not knowing any Spanish, except a few single words, we improvised as we went along. I knew sign language, and I used this form of communication along with gestures and exaggerated facial expressions in an attempt to convey my words or meaning. I had a small card with some Spanish phrases printed on it, and I quickly learned these phrases. "Hello friend, what is your name?, goodbye, good evening, you are very pretty, please, thank you, girl, boy, mother, father, home, I'm lost and I'm with Jack's group."

Occasionally, one of the volunteers in our group who spoke Spanish would stop his work to interpret for me something that I wanted the children to know or something that the children wanted me to understand.

I wondered why everything stunk, and I finally turned to a little girl sitting beside me. Tapping her on the shoulder, I plugged my nose with two fingers while making a face, then put my hands out, palms up, hoping I was communicating, "Why does it stink so badly?" The children began to giggle, "What?" I asked. Then they, too, plugged their noses and pointed beneath my outstretched legs as I saw a sporadic trail of bowel movements silently floating by in the trickling water that the children had played in.

That week, my 49-year-old body became their jungle gym. One little girl clung to my legs until I agreed to pick her up and carry her on my hip until I could no longer do it. One middle-aged girl scolded the little girl for insisting she ride on my hip. The little girl cried and put all ten fingers in her mouth. Then, as tears, spit, and snot mingled together, she flung both arms around my neck. The middle-sized children argued among themselves over whose turn it was to hold my hand or put their arms through mine. Day after day, they struggled to see who was the quickest to find a place by my side as they literally plastered their little bodies next to mine. Later, I realized as we walked, they had matched their step to mine. I did a quick double step, and they looked surprised and giggled. Then, they did the same, and I followed them. We had fun! The older boys followed behind as they were too cool to take up with silly girls, but they stayed near me all week. Sometimes, I would start singing, and the kids sang something in Spanish. We would clap and march as we traveled up one road and down another. Other times, I'd skip, and soon all would be skipping and laughing. I started playing a hand game with gibberish words, and I was fascinated by how closely the children watched the movement of my lips, listening until they realized it wasn't any language at all, just a bunch of funny sounds. They memorized them quickly.

I became known as the Pied Piper, an entertainer of the children and returning them to their parents at the end of each day. Our little group grew in numbers. My heart was happy as every morning when we arrived, children were either waiting or they came running. By the end of the day, my body was exhausted. Then they stood in line to play my funny hand game with me, which we played over and over until I thought they would never stop!

One day, the children took my hand and led me down a dirt road. I wondered where they were taking me, but I couldn't think of a way to ask that question, so I let them lead me on. On the way, we played "follow the leader," and one by one, we twirled, danced, and jumped our way along the dusty path as we went farther and farther away from the construction site.

We walked for a long time in the sweltering heat before we finally reached their destination, a basketball court. The girls and I sat in the shade as the boys tried to make baskets with rocks. I was their cheering section, and I clapped them on while the girls quietly talked among themselves and braided my hair. I noticed an older group of boys who I hadn't seen before had appeared on the court. I had been distracted by what the girls were doing to my hair and was startled to hear a fight break out. I was stunned when I realized they were throwing rocks at one another as hard as they could. One of our boys was crying; I feared he had been hit with a rock. I didn't know what to do, and I panicked. I jumped up and ran, placing my body, arms held high, between the two that were now fighting with their fists. Realizing I had nothing to say to stop them, I got scared and quickly backed away.

Grabbing the girls, we ran from the court as I angrily yelled over my shoulder as loudly as I could, "Amigos, no! Amigos, no!"

I continued yelling this over and over as we quickly walked on. I hoped the boys would realize we had suddenly left and would follow. I didn't know if the older boys would follow them and keep fighting, and this made me nervous. It was the first time I realized how helpless I was in their country when I couldn't communicate. Then I saw a group of old men watching us. They had witnessed the fight and said nothing. They had seen me jump between the two boys and offered no help. They had heard it all and yet sat there, as if watching TV; they never budged. They wore smirks on their faces, and I felt evil was nearby. I had no idea where I was going, but I was angry. Clearly, it was me leading the group of children now. I wanted to quickly get away from the uncomfortable eyes of those men, and I wanted those children back near the construction site, closer to their homes. But as I walked in haste with them, trying to keep up with me, I had no idea how to get back to the site, as every gravel road looked the same. Later, I realized as I was leading the children away, they, too, were leading me back to safety as they silently turned down one road and then another as I continued believing I was leading them to safety.

The following day, one of the builders loaned me his Polaroid camera, and I took dozens of pictures of children who then stood proudly with their photo in hand as they admired themselves. I asked the children to show me their homes. I pointed to one child at a time as I signed and spoke in Spanish, "Where is your Casa?" as I looked around in all directions. The kids understood exactly what I was asking, and one at a time, each took me to see their home, where I met their mother, grandmother, or whoever was inside. I took pictures of each child standing in front of their home, smiling proudly as their family stood beside them. When a few of the mothers who lived close together realized what I was doing, one held up her finger, which I understood to mean, "Wait a minute," or "I'll be right back," as they ran off each into their own home. Before I knew it, they reappeared dressed in their fanciest dresses and shoes. These clothes were dated and looked worn out. They had combed their hair or pulled it back into a knot, and on their lips, they wore bright red lipstick. I made a "La-de-da" expression by putting my hand on my hip and puckering my lips. The women laughed then and spoke their names to me in Spanish. I repeated their names and asked how old they were by holding up my ten fingers, closing both fists, and opening them up again and again. When I reached my age, I pointed to myself. The women then began to tell me their ages by using their hands, opening and closing their fists, and counting individual fingers to count off their age. Luckily, I knew the numbers one to ten in Spanish, as that helped. I was shocked when one of the women told me she too was 49, my age, as I would have guessed her to be at least seventy-five, her face and body weathered by the sun and the hard life that accompanies living in a dump. (I do not use this word as a negative; it's what it was.) After the family pictures were distributed, the mothers hugged me, and a few invited me into their homes.

In one child's home, I was instructed to sit at a small table, and out came a torn checkerboard with a few checkers. We played checkers as the grandfather and a chicken lay on a mattress on the floor beside us. This home consisted of two rooms, the kitchen and the bedroom; both rooms had dirt floors. It was tiny but neat except for the brown filth on the bed. I noticed a cross hung by the door, and a Spanish Bible was on the floor near the mattress. In the next home, I was offered a cold orange drink as gratitude for the pictures. Jack had warned us not to drink the water as we would likely become ill. Yet I knew the gratitude this woman was showing me, so I kindly accepted her orange drink and took a little sip; it was Tang. I quickly decided it should be shared by everyone because everyone was hot and thirsty. So, the drink passed around the room until it was gone. While this gentle kindness was going on inside the house, an angry-looking man stood outside the house, snapping a thick black whip onto the ground, watching me. Feeling uncomfortable, I thanked the mother and the rest of the kids, and I left. When we were far enough away from the angry man, I turned to one of the middle-aged girls and, using my face and expressions, tried to communicate, "What's up with him?" The girl seemed to understand as she shrugged her shoulders and talked on and on in Spanish. Occasionally, she'd turn back to look at him, shaking her head as she talked on.

The women were proud of their homes despite the dirt floors and the stench they lived in. They were polite, friendly, and welcoming to me. Crosses or worn pictures of Jesus hung on cardboard walls. Perhaps they knew nothing different, such as tiles for flooring or carpet. They had done the best they could with the little they had, and they made good homes to raise their children in. I was in awe of their tenacity and their ability to survive this way of life, but what struck me the most was how happy they all were. They were dealing with their life challenges as we all do, despite the enormous hardships that surrounded them. Husbands and wives were parenting and raising their children in the homes they had made. They were amazing, as I thought I could never do what they had been doing forever. Several times during the week, I noticed a woman off to the side, standing alone, not talking or laughing with the other women. When this lady spoke, she waved her hands, and her voice came out too loud as if she couldn't hear herself. Of course! She was deaf.

Towards the end of the week, the deaf woman appeared at the construction site. One of the builders who spoke Spanish stopped what he was doing and tried to communicate with her. Then he told me he thought she wanted to see the dentist but was afraid and wanted me to go with her. I nodded, "Okay, I will go," she smiled at me then, showing me a full mouth of rotten teeth. When we arrived, there was a long line of people waiting to see the doctor, nurses, and dentists. I felt bad as I politely and gently pushed my way through the crowd, saying, "Gracias," until we reached the reception area, where I told a lady behind the desk about the deaf woman needing to see the dentist. The receptionist told me that would be impossible because all these people were ahead of her and that the children had priority over all the adults. I didn't know what to do. If we went to the back of the line, she would never be seen. The reception area was filled with people whose bodies stunk from hours of standing outside in the hot sun and perhaps in clothes that had not been washed for a while. The smell, along with the lack of air movement in the clinic, made me slightly nauseated. I found a chair for the deaf woman and told her I was going to find Jack.

It was near the end of the day, nearly time for the clinic to close, and this was Friday, our last day. I was afraid I would not be able to find Jack in time for the deaf woman to be seen by the dentist. Each person I asked told me Jack had just left and was going to the school. At the school, I ran down the long hallway through the first floor, no Jack. Running up the steps, I ran down the long hallway of the second floor, still no Jack. Taking two steps at a time to the third floor, I ran down the hall and finally found a woman who told me Jack was on the roof. I ran up one more flight of steps, and there Jack was, talking and eating with a group of people. I was literally jumping up and down with nervous impatience and apologizing for my rude interruption as I quickly explained the dilemma. Jack excused us and swiftly led the way back down three flights of stairs and across the walk into the clinic he went to. I could barely keep up with him!

Jack spoke in Spanish to several people in the reception area who were preparing to shut down the clinic, and then I heard him say in English, "This deaf woman has wanted to come here all week but was too frightened; we must make time to see her." Maybe he had said the same in Spanish. She was the last person to be seen that day as the others were told to return home. I motioned for the deaf lady to follow me as I followed Jack back to the dental office. I felt like I'd stepped back in time as I walked into a crowded dental room right out of the nineteen sixties. The small room had two dental chairs with worn, torn, plastic linings and what looked like old-fashioned dental instruments. The other dentist was working on a little boy who was screaming at the top of his lungs as he tried to get out of the dental chair. The people around him were speaking to him in Spanish, but the little guy would not listen; he just kept on screaming. The other dentist, his assistant, the deaf woman, and I all stood a foot apart, looking at one another in the hot, overcrowded room as we watched the scene of the screaming child. The dentist then instructed the deaf woman to sit. She hesitated, and I signed for her to sit. A dull headache was beginning to form in the back of my eyes as the child kept screaming. Turning towards the dentist, I mumbled, "At least she can't hear him." He nodded. I made sure the deaf woman was fine before I weaved my way back through the bodies towards the exit door, saying, "Excuse me," four times as at least four bodies inched one way and then the other to let me pass when Jack suddenly opened the door and stuck his head inside to see how we were doing. Then he looked at me as I was about to leave and suggested I stay with the deaf woman until she was done. So once again, I said, "Excuse me," four more times as all the bodies hunched over the boy inched aside once again, allowing me to pass by. The deaf woman looked nervous, so I leaned towards her and squeezed her hand, nodding an expression that I hoped looked like encouragement. I stood at the dentist's right side, which was at the foot of the dental chair, so she could see me if that made her feel better. I looked around the small room. Paint was peeling off the walls and ceiling, "Someone needs to paint bright colors with pictures in here so kids could look at something fun and not be so scared," I said as I looked at all the bodies hovering over the child who had now agreed to open his mouth, allowing the dentist to look inside.

There was no air movement in the room, no air-conditioner; it was stiflingly hot. I looked at the dentist and his assistant, realizing they had been working all day in this stuffy, overheated, claustrophobic room. Sweat was dripping down their brows and dripping off their noses, and their clothes hung damp on their bodies like wet clothes hung across a clothesline. I took a deep breath and leaned back against the wall; the entire room smelled of sweat. Looking at the deaf woman, I noticed she had worn what was probably her best dress while her hands fidgeted in her lap. In the heat of the day, I hadn't noticed how she was dressed while we trekked down the hill to the clinic. I was exhausted from the week, but surprised by how sad I felt as tomorrow we were leaving. In the stiflingly hot room, I could hardly breathe as I wondered what I was doing in this overcrowded, overheated dentist's office. After all, it wasn't as if the deaf, Spanish-speaking woman and I were going to have a conversation. I have never handled the sight of blood without fainting, and anything remotely smelly that oozes out of bodily orifices turns my stomach. As I looked at the dental team only inches away, the air between us was blurred as heat and sweat came at me like an ocean coming onto the shore. The dentist presumed I would be signing in Spanish as he began speaking to the deaf woman in Spanish.

I gave him a little jab in his ribs with my elbow and said, "Hey doc, you're going to have to speak English to me because I don't know any Spanish." I wondered what the dentist and nurse's assistants thought. Frankly, I was still wondering what I was doing there, signing English to a deaf woman who signed in homemade Spanish. The dentist said to the deaf woman, "Open your mouth." So in English, I signed, "Open your mouth." The deaf woman was hesitant to open her mouth and looked scared, so I leaned toward her and gave her hand a friendly little pat. I nodded my head for her to do as the dentist instructed, and then I signed and spoke aloud in English, "It's okay, it's alright," so at least the dentist knew what I was saying, even if the deaf woman couldn't hear me or understand American Sign Language (ASL).

During the dentist's examination, I stood at the deaf woman's feet, watching her expressions as she kept her eyes on me. Periodically, I reassured her by signing, "It's okay, it's alright," whenever she suddenly jumped or shifted in the chair. After the dentist finished examining her teeth, he explained to her in English, while I signed in English, "You have an infected tooth in the front of your mouth. That tooth needs to be extracted so the gum around the tooth can heal." He told her, "It's badly infected, which is the reason it hurts." The deaf woman began to sign back, and I reversed what she was signing by verbally speaking her words to the dentist. "No, please," she signed, "I don't want my tooth pulled." But the dentist answered back, "If you don't allow me to pull that tooth, the infection will come back," and I signed this in English back to her. The deaf woman signed back to the dentist, "Can't you give me some medicine that will make the pain go away?" and once again, I reversed her signs by verbally asking the dentist her question. The dentist replied, "Yes, I will give you some medication for the infection, but the infection will come back. It would be best if you allowed me to remove the tooth, ending the pain and the problem." I signed in English to the deaf woman what the dentist had said. The deaf woman signed back, "No, I do not want my tooth pulled, no, no, no, just fix it please, and I'll take the medication. It will get better on its own." In English, I spoke the words to the dentist that the deaf Spanish woman had signed to me. The dentist replied, "Okay, if you're sure that's what you want, but it's not what I would recommend." I signed in English, "Okay, if you're sure that's what you want, but it's not what I would recommend." The deaf woman smiled and happily signed back, "Yes, that is what I want. I don't want my tooth pulled. That would look bad, and I would no longer be attractive." I spoke the words she signed, telling the dentist what she said. The dentist then asked her name. I signed, "What is your name?" The deaf woman spelled out her name, and I reversed what she spelled and verbally told the dentist her name. Then the dentist asked the deaf woman if she had any children. I signed his question in English, "Do you have any children?" The deaf Spanish woman signed back, saying, "Yes, two," and she held up two fingers. The dentist asked what her husband would want her to do about her tooth, and in English, I signed his question to the deaf Spanish woman. The deaf woman signed back to me, "I have no husband. I had a boyfriend, but he ran off with some other woman," she shrugged her shoulders. I verbally spoke what the deaf woman had signed so the dentist could understand her reply. The dentist explained that he would clean out the infection the best he could. I signed his verbal statement to her, and she signed, "Okay." I said to the dentist, "Okay." The dentist said, "Open wide." I signed in English, "Open wide." The deaf woman opened her mouth as wide as she could, and after a few seconds, she began to ask in sign language, "What is the bad taste?" I reversed her question and asked the dentist, "What is the bad taste?" He said, and I signed, "It's the pus from the infection, I'm cleaning it out." I caught a glance of the huge hole in the woman's gums as smelly green pus oozed out and down her chin.

Instantly, I felt faint. I tried to keep my eyes focused on the deaf woman's eyes, but I could still see a glimpse of the hole in her gums, and it was gigantic. I began to feel nauseated; sweat was pouring down my back and between my breasts. Fearing I was about to throw up, I leaned back against the wall and closed my eyes, silently praying, "Help me, God, help me hang on; this is not the time to be weak or faint." It seemed I leaned into the wall for hours while the dentist silently worked to clean out the infection until eventually, I heard the dentist say he was finished, and I came alive and signed, "All finished," as his assistant handed the deaf woman some medication. The nurse told the deaf woman how much medication to take and how often to take it. I signed her instructions to the deaf woman. The deaf woman was so pleased she nearly jumped out of the chair, and she was beaming as she signed, "All finished?" The dentist and his assistant nodded, and the dentist said in English, "All finished!" I again signed, "All finished!" With a big smile spread across her face, she jumped out of the dental chair and bounced out of the room as both dentists and their assistants looked towards me. "We didn't think you were going to make it," they said, "you were white as a sheet the entire time!"

I left the clinic in a daze and wandered up the hill to the construction site. The heat was stifling. Even though it was beastly hot outside, it felt cooler outside than in the dental office, where no breeze blew. I walked slowly up the hill. I don't recall climbing into the van for the last time or saying goodbye to the children, but on the drive back to our hotel, I closed my eyes and rested my head; it was pounding. I dozed off. I was too exhausted to speak. Once we arrived at our hotel room, I climbed into bed, unsure if I would ever get out again. It wasn't until our nightly group meeting that my exhaustion lifted, and my intellect seemed to kick in. I began to realize what had happened. I couldn't wait to share my experience with the other volunteers, and I wanted answers. I asked them, "How did that work? She was deaf and spoke and signed in Spanish?" No one spoke, so I continued, "I was signing in English, and what I saw coming back to me was her signing in perfect English! The entire thing is impossible!" I explained exasperatedly. "And I don't know why I didn't realize that at the time?" Stillness settled over the room as tears slid down my cheeks. My tired mind succumbed to my intellectual desire to understand how it was possible that, at that moment in time, there were suddenly no communication barriers between a deaf Spanish-speaking woman and a hearing English-speaking woman. "We have a lot of miracles here," Jack said, smiling.

"The blind receive sight, the lame walk, those who have leprosy are cleansed, the deaf hear, the dead are raised, and the good news is proclaimed to the poor. Blessed is anyone who does not stumble on account of me."

Matthew 11:5-6

"Then Jesus said to his disciples: 'Therefore I tell you, do not worry about your life, what you will eat; or about your body, what you will wear. For life is more than food, and the body more than clothes. Consider the ravens: They do not sow or reap, they have no storeroom or barn; yet God feeds them. And how much more valuable are you than birds! Who of you by worrying can add a single hour to your life?'"

Luke 12:22-25

THOUGHTS

When I returned from the Dominican Republic, it was quite a shock. For the first time, I realized how very little I needed to live. I certainly didn't need a cell phone, or any phone for that matter; none of the Dominicans had a computer other than the one at the home where the pastor resided. I didn't need one of those to survive. None of the Dominicans had TVs or any electronic gadgets. What I realized is that I basically need a change of clothing while the first one is scrubbed clean; no washer or dryer. I didn't need make-up, or a perm, or a car, or a home; little money is needed to live in the Dominican Republic. I realized it was much like the TV show where the players also have to make their make-shift home out of bamboo and ropes, natural elements woven together, and start a fire with the use of flint and natural materials. Their environment was thatched roofs with no walls. They, too, were very often hungry, which is a foreign concept for most middle-class Americans who live in a home with a roof and walls. Once I'd returned to my life back home, it was a long time before I purchased anything other than food and paid my monthly bills. I was filled with the awareness of want versus need and tried to live more according to the need factor. As time went on, like everything else, I was pulled back into my American standards and needed yet another pair of shoes to add to the 20 pairs I already had! Then came the extra clothes and the belief that what I really needed was a new car, as my present one was already a few years old. How spoiled I am! How spoiled we all are! I do try to thank God for all these extras and that I was lucky to be born in America, where many people live with full stomachs, clothing, and shelter (let alone cushy motor vehicles). I also failed to pray this prayer of thanksgiving, or even remember it, due to my busy life, that is, until the turkey was cut and placed in the middle of a beautifully set table with places for all to sit. Then I remember.

CHAPTER 8

A Greeting from My Ancestors

WINTER 2003

The year was 2003, and it was early Christmas morning. I was lying in bed, and I had just opened my eyes. There before me were my great aunt and uncle, Ed and Emma, my paternal grandparents, Nemo and Grandpa, and my maternal grandparents, Grammy and Grampy-Red. I recognized them immediately! Each of them was a small circular sphere of energy that was shimmering love towards me, yet within one larger circular sphere, that also shimmered loving energy.

Instantly, I propped myself up on my elbow as tears of joy rolled down my cheeks. I thought, "Hi guys, what are you all doing here?" My mind received their loving message in response, "Hi Krissy, it's Christmas morning, and we're here to check on you!" "Krissy," the only name my Grampy-Red ever called me. I felt waves of enormous love and wishes for a Merry Christmas emanating from the energy spheres, both the large circular sphere and the three smaller ones that were my family members who had passed on decades prior. Seconds later, they were gone, disappearing into thin air. I was without words and amazed at what had just happened. I recognized I had just received the best Christmas gift I could have ever been given: a visit from my dead ancestors! It was a euphoric, loved, "peace beyond all human understanding," kind of experience. I felt overjoyed!

"He is the one you praise; he is your God who performed for you those great and awesome wonders you saw with your own eyes."

Deuteronomy 10:21

THOUGHTS

I know how far out this sounds; it's bizarre. One thing I have learned as a therapist in counseling others is that the truth is stranger than fiction, but it's completely true. Whether you believe it or not is up to you. No one can force you to believe if it doesn't sit well with you. And in this world, we should be discerning and cautious.

I don't have a tapestry of thoughts to share about this spiritual experience, as it lasted about 10-15 seconds only. I will never make anything up to fill a void, so it is what it was.

CHAPTER 9

The Glass Spoon

FALL 2005

Although I've made many mistakes in my life, one of the bigger ones was getting remarried in 2003. After my twenty-six-year marriage ended in divorce, I waited for the recommended two years before I became involved with anyone. Then I turned to a Christian Internet Site to find what I prayed for: a holy man, a Godly man, and the first man I met seemed wonderful. I did not realize just how naive I was or catch just how starved I was for attention, let alone love. After all the spiritual experiences I'd had, I simply believed this was just another one and that God was granting me this man as a gift for my trying to work out my first marriage for so long. After knowing this man for three months, I married him, something I would never have advised anyone to do, but I believed he was a gift from God. I thought to myself, " How could I go wrong in marrying him sooner versus later?" He was from Florida, and I loved Florida. I planned to move there following my youngest daughter's graduation from high school, which was two years later. Until then, I was flying back and forth between South Dakota and Florida for one week each month. I was crazy about him, and it was an exciting time in my life!

I informed all my clients of my upcoming move and closed my counseling practice of twenty-four years. I gave my car to my daughter and son-in-law. I sold all my furniture, winter clothes, dishes, washer and dryer, lawn mower, shovels, snow blower, desks, and beds. I sold or threw away 30 years of everything I owned and spent hundreds of dollars on bubble wrap, styrofoam peanuts, boxes, and packing tape for the marriage I believed was a gift from God.

That Spring and Summer of 2005, I walked the small town I had lived in for the past 16 years, and said all my goodbyes to the small-town life and people I'd come to cherish. I hired a moving company that drove my boxed-up life to Florida. In the meantime, I had spent a lot of time in the air. I had flown to Florida for a week out of every month to be with my new husband. It was at 35,000 feet and less than six months into the marriage that I had to come clean and admit to myself that I'd made a big mistake. I didn't love him. I knew now I had moved too fast into this promise of a relationship. However, true to my nature, I tried to work it out until finally, in year number two, I filed for divorce. Within 60 days, I was once again a divorced woman. It was a marriage I am not proud of. It was embarrassing, a mistake on my part not to get to know this man before I happily jumped back into a sacred union where I longed to be loved and cared for. Some situations began to occur that I would not tolerate, and I knew a divorce was imminent. I believed in the institution of marriage, and I wanted to be married again. I wanted my husband to be my best friend and my soulmate. I wanted to be loved for who I was, not what I had. So I made the marriage happen.

I had emotionally tricked myself into believing this was God's will for my future. But this is what happens when people take their life back from God. When I took my life back from God, my life fell apart. God did not make this marriage happen as I had wanted to believe. I made it happen. Unknowingly, I took back control of my life instead of giving it up to God. I had a lot to learn about trusting the Lord, patience and discernment!

I hired the same moving company to move my already packed and boxed-up life back to the Midwest. I had no winter clothes. I had no car. I had no office. I had no furniture. Diane opened her home to me, and I lived with Diane and her husband, Dave, for six months until I found a condo I could buy. My boxed-up life waiting in storage. My kids gave me my car back, and a fellow therapist opened her counseling practice to me. I began to see clients again. Little did my clients know, I was a client myself as I sought the wisdom and emotional support of my former psychologist, Dr. Doug Anderson, in Sioux Falls, South Dakota. I had been through a lot, and I needed to heal.

"The simple believe anything, but the prudent give thought to their steps" (Proverbs 14:15).

Two days prior to Christmas of 2005, I moved into my condo. Several of my close friends met me at the condo to unload the van filled with my boxes. Once the van was empty, my garage was full of stacked boxes four to five feet high. It took me weeks to go through every box. Slowly, bedding, dishes, pictures, and books reappeared and found a place within my new home. However, my garage now held all the empty boxes, which were tossed about among mounds of Styrofoam peanuts and bubble wrap hung together by packing tape. My garage was a giant mess! This didn't bother me, knowing it would eventually get hauled to the dump, until I discovered I was missing a tiny glass spoon, and I do mean tiny, it is 2 & 1/2 inches long and 1/2 of an inch wide!

I had been returning my antique cup collection and cut-glass platters, bowls, vases, sugars, and creamers back into my antique China cabinet when I noticed the tiny glass spoon that belonged to the tiny cut-glass sugar and creamer set wasn't there. My stomach sank knowing it was lost somewhere in the mound of boxes, bubble wrap, tape, and a garage full of Styrofoam peanuts!

I remembered wrapping it up. I wrapped it very carefully, circling the spoon with layers of bubble wrap over and over; it was so fragile and small. It was such a sweet little spoon. I felt so bad. I had to find that spoon, Nemo had given it to me with the miniature cut-glass sugar and creamer set.

It took me a few weeks before I could even make myself look for it, as the very thought of it seemed utterly impossible. I knew what I was going to have to sort through was equivalent to searching for a needle in a haystack. I looked at the mess covering my garage floor that was several feet deep as I walked through the path each day, in and out of my garage to my car parked outside. I knew I couldn't begin to clean it all up until I had turned the garage inside out in order to find that glass spoon. Otherwise, I knew it would get tossed out with the rest of the mess, no one ever knowing a tiny treasure was hidden somewhere within the city dump.

One morning, I felt ready to search for my tiny spoon. I was surprised at how optimistic I felt about it. However, as I surveyed the garage from where I stood in the middle of it, my optimism dropped. I said a prayer to Saint Anthony. (A Catholic Saint who is called for when something has been lost.) "Tony, Tony, come around, something is lost that must be found." Then I prayed to God that if it was His will, I would find that little treasure. I stood for about five minutes in the middle of the mess, not knowing which way to turn; my garage was filled in every direction with trash. I prayed about it and tried to remain open to the Spirit's lead and not think. "Just feel," I told myself over and over, "Just feel, just feel." Suddenly, I knew exactly where the glass spoon was, and I walked over to the northwest corner of the garage and started to pick through handfuls of bubble wrap, masking tape, and boxes full of peanuts. Tossing them all aside, I reached for a specific chunk of bubble wrap that was tucked inside a box, and using my fingers, I felt around the edges of that particular chunk of bubble wrap until I felt the slight outline of a tiny spoon! I jumped up and down in my garage! I got scissors and carefully started to snip away at the taped edges of the wrapping. After all this, I didn't want to break the spoon in half! I am known for overwrapping and over-taping everything, so there I sat on my garage floor, surrounded by more of the same, as I carefully cut my way through the many layers of protection that I had padded around it before its journey to Florida and back. Finally, I saw my little glass spoon at the bottom of the wrapped layers.

I was overjoyed and couldn't believe I had found the tiny spoon, and I said a prayer of thanksgiving to Saint Anthony and God for leading me to the tiny glass spoon, truly hidden, like a needle in a haystack.

"For we live by faith, not by sight."

2 Corinthians 5:7

THOUGHTS

Instead of me trying to make sense out of this, my mom gave me this writing by John Henry Newman following my second divorce. I believe it explains my situation very well.

Trust Your Shepherd:

"God has determined, unless I interfere with his plan, that I should reach that which will be my greatest happiness. He looks at me individually, he calls me by my name, he knows what I can do, what I can best be, what is my greatest happiness, and he means to give it to me.

God knows what is my greatest happiness, but I do not. There is no rule about what is happy and good; what suits one would not suit another. And the ways by which perfection is reached vary very much; the medicines necessary for our souls are very different from each other. Thus God leads us in strange ways. We know he wills our happiness, but we neither know what our happiness is nor the way. We are blind. Left to ourselves, we would take the wrong way; we must leave it to him. Let us put ourselves into his hands and not be startled even though he leads us by a strange way....Let us be sure he will lead us right, that he will bring us to that which is, not indeed what we think best, nor what is best for another, but what is best for us."[1]

"Know that the Lord is God. It is he who made us, and we are his; we are his people, the sheep of his pasture."

Psalm 100:3

---

[1] Newman, John Henry. *Meditations and Devotions*. "Meditations IX." *The Newman Reader*, 6 Mar. 1848, www.newmanreader.org/works/meditations/meditations9.html

CHAPTER 10

Healing My Knee

WINTER 2006

In the winter of 2006, in the middle of a stormy winter day, I got my car stuck in the snow. No one was around to help me, so I tried to push the car out myself. In pushing my car backward, I slipped, and my right knee hit the top edge of the license plate. The pain was unbearable! I hunched over a pile of snow in pain, trying to catch my breath. Some boys from down the street saw me lying in a snowbank and came to help me get my car out of the snow. However, my knee was hurting badly, and I didn't know what to do about it. I was late for a counseling appointment at my office, so I pushed the pain back in my mind and refused to pay attention to it. After my appointment was done, I pulled up the leg of my pants to look at my knee; it was swollen, and I could see it was forming a substantial bruise.

It hurt to walk, so I hopped. I hopped to my car and drove over to my friend's office, where she is a Certified Nurse Practitioner. I asked her to look at my knee. After examining it, she concluded that I might have torn my meniscus. The meniscus is made up of two tough pieces of cartilage that rest between the thigh bone and the shin bone. With this diagnosis, I hopped back to the car and went home. In doing so, my car got stuck in the snow in my driveway. It had been a stressful day, and I was in a lot of pain; I started to cry.

Not knowing what else to do, I called my son-in-law to come to help me, and he called his father to help him. They used two large shovels, and it took them 20 minutes to free my car from the compacted snow, allowing me to drive into the garage. When they came into the house to tell me goodbye, I asked my son-in-law's father, Tony, who is a chiropractor and friend of mine, to look at my knee. He looked at my knee and said, "Oh wow, Kris, you've probably torn your meniscus." Now, I'd never heard of a meniscus before today, but it had achieved a new level of pain, and it had swollen bigger than it was in the afternoon.

After they left, I crawled on the floor on my hands and one knee to the dining room table. I had to use my toes from the leg that was injured to push myself along, and it hurt. I pulled out a chair from the dining room table and crawled up so I was now leaning onto the back of the chair. I moved the chair forward one step with my arms, and I hopped one step. I moved the chair ahead one more step, and I hopped another step and moved the chair one more step forward. I did this until I made it into my bedroom where I rested my injured leg on the chair while undressing for bed.

This was not an easy feat! I had an antique bed, and it was very high. To get into it, I had to place pressure on my injured leg.

The pain was unbearable! I placed the chair alongside my bed and crawled in. I was hungry, but there was no way I was going to be able to get back to the other end of my house, where my kitchen was, in order to fix something to eat. My knee, now swollen twice its size, was purple and very painful. As I sat on the edge of my bed, I began to think, "What was I going to do?" I had no spouse to help me. I was on my own with this, and I couldn't even help myself. I couldn't even go get myself crutches. How was I going to carry on with work, getting dressed, buying groceries, and all the things one does to get ready for the day and keep up a house and job?

Suddenly, I knew what to do. With the help of the chair, I hopped into my office, where I had a cross hanging on the wall. The cross had hidden inside it two vials of precious oil that Abbot David Geraets had prayed over and given to me at the Monastery. I had never used it.

Without a thought about whether this would work, I believed wholeheartedly that God would heal my knee. I had no doubts about it and no questioning thoughts of, "I hope this works." While rubbing the oil onto my knee, I prayed for Jesus to heal me. I knew God would heal my knee. I felt it. I prayed and rubbed the oil into my knee, and then crawled into bed and went to sleep. I slept soundly, and when I woke up, I got out of bed before I was fully awake. Then I remembered my injured knee. I looked at my knee. There was nothing there! No bruises! It was not swollen, not even a scratch. It didn't hurt. It wasn't sore. I could run, walk, and jump up and down. And I did! It was as though it never happened at all. God answered my prayer as I believed He would.

"Ask and it will be given to you; seek and you will find; knock and the door will be opened to you. For everyone who asks receives; the one who seeks finds; and to the one who knocks, the door will be opened."

Matthew 7:7-8

"Therefore I say to you, whatever things you ask when you pray, believe that you receive *them*, and you will have *them*."

Mark 11:24, NKJV

"I tell you the truth, anyone who doesn't receive the Kingdom of God like a child will never enter it."

Mark 10:15, NLT

"If any of you lacks wisdom, let him ask God, who gives generously to all without reproach, and it will be given to him. But let him ask in faith, with no doubting, for the one who doubts is like a wave of the sea that is driven and tossed by the wind. For that person must not suppose that he will receive anything from the Lord; he is a double minded man, unstable in all his ways."

James 1:5-8, ESV

Thoughts

My only way of understanding this miracle is to say I believed as a child would, not doubting or even questioning if this would work. To this day, I continue to be astonished that it never entered my adult mind, nor did I ever wonder if it would work. I was pure and filled with the childlike knowledge that I would be healed. And I was! I jumped up and down and I hollered, "Thank you, Jesus!"

CHAPTER 11

The Nudge

SUMMER 2010

I've had other opportunities to do God's will. There are times I've felt God's nudges, but I hesitated, and the opportunity was lost on my nervousness or not wanting to draw attention to myself. I sadly recall an incident at a store one day. I was going through the checkout line, and I was just about to write my check when I noticed an elderly woman standing in line behind me. I felt the "nudge." She had only a few personal items, and her presence became significant to me. Somehow, I knew money was a shortage for her, and again, I felt that "nudge" that said, "Tell the woman at the cash register you'll be paying for her items too." But I didn't.

I was afraid I'd hear angel wings flapping and that I would collapse with tears of joy right there in the store in front of other people. I feel ashamed of myself for not following that "nudge" in my mind to pay for the women's few items. I have asked for God's forgiveness, and I know I've been forgiven, yet I will always regret not listening to God's goodness.

So, how come? I wonder, "Why would God speak to me anyway?" Most people know the Bible better than I do. I haven't even read the entire Bible for Heaven's sake, and there are thousands of people who have committed their lives to serving God through spiritual study and missionary work, so why me, an ordinary woman?

When I was a kid in Sunday school, my teachers had to bribe me to learn the Ten Commandments. They bribed me with quarters. I made a quarter each time I memorized a Commandment and earned two dollars and fifty cents from the Commandments alone! That doesn't sound like much money for the year of two thousand twenty-five, but in the early sixties, it was a lot of money for a kid. Between memorizing the Ten Commandments, the Affirmation of Faith, the Apostles Creed, and some of the books of the Bible, I earned a bunch of cash! I didn't mind getting up early Sunday mornings, knowing I was going to get paid. Evidently, one Sunday school teacher along the way decided I needed some extra incentive to do the memorization work, and with each passing year, every new teacher continued what the first had begun.

I do recall how angry and embarrassed my parents were when they discovered I was getting paid to learn what every other good Lutheran child learned without getting paid. When I recall my childhood days and how oppositional I attempted to be, and my adult years of believing that I was the master of my own life, I find it astounding that God would speak to me, an ordinary woman and daughter of the King of Kings.

———————————

"Give generously to them and do so without a grudging heart; then because of this the Lord your God will bless you in all your work and in everything you put your hand to. There will always be poor people in the land. Therefore I command you to be openhanded toward your fellow Is-raelites who are poor and needy in the land."

Deuteronomy 15:10-11

"Then Jesus said to his host, 'When you give a luncheon or dinner, do not invite your friends, your brothers or sis-ters, your relatives, or your rich neighbor; if you do, they may invite you back and so you will be repaid. But when you give a banquet, invite the poor, the crippled, the lame, the blind, and you will be blessed. Although they cannot repay you, you will be repaid at the resurrection of the righteous."

Luke 14:12-14

THOUGHTS

I wish I had listened to that " nudge!" Better to fall on my knees in a store and to cry tears of joy and to hear angel wings than disobey Jesus. I pray often that God will help me be more considerate of others and not so concerned with myself, and for the forgiveness of all my sins.

I believe Abbot David Geraets spoke God's truth when he said, "Her life will never be the same."

CHAPTER 12

Holy Whispers

MARCH 2019

The dolphin appeared out of nowhere! Diane, Mary, and I walked along the beach in the Bonita Springs area of Florida along the Gulf of Mexico. Suddenly, there she was! A small dolphin was swimming in the shallow waters along the beach where we walked. The dolphin swam at the exact pace we walked. We watched the dolphin arch into the air, swim under the surface, and arch over and over again. It was a magnificent sight and we were absolutely speechless!

It was the third week in March of 2019, and we three friends had just disembarked the pontoon that took us across the bay and through the mangroves to the Gulf of Mexico. Mom had dementia, then a fall and a broken hip. She began a period of not eating. Two weeks after her fall, she died of starvation, and her spirit went to Jesus at noon on March 1st, 2018. For the past year, I had been praying to God for a sign that Mom was still with me. I knew she was in heaven, but I missed her deeply. In life, Mom and I promised one another that whoever died first would come back to the one left behind, if possible. I wanted it to be possible. I believed it was possible!

Diane, Mary, and I carried our beach chairs on our backs and a cooler pack of food for a day in the sun. Other people were near us, but no one hollered and no one pointed, "Hey look, there's a dolphin!" as people usually do. Time felt different; I felt confused. My mind scrambled to understand this feeling, but I could not. I could only experience it. Was I in a memory? Mom swam with a dolphin at Discovery Cove in Orlando, Florida, in 2005. It was my Christmas gift to her. My two siblings, David and Arne, and I have a picture of Mom kissing the dolphin at the end of her swim. The ocean and dolphins were her favorite things.

Suddenly, Mary said, "I wonder if that's Jone?" Behind my sunglasses, I began a silent weep. I had wondered that, too. I wanted to believe it was my mom! I missed my mom! When I feel a yearning to talk with my mother about something that is bigger than me, I've had one dream that repeats night after night, week after week, or month after month. In my dream, I am trying to call my mother. It is set in the time after my parents had divorced, and my mother lived in a home my brother purchased for her. No matter how hard I try, I can not remember her phone number! In my dream, I would enlist other people for their help in figuring out my mother's phone number, which never occurred. In my unconscious state of sleep, I was searching for my mother, and it has been my recurring dream for seven years.

The dolphin followed us as we walked along the beach's edge

for maybe one minute. That dolphin swam about ten feet from where we walked, and somehow, it kept the slow pace of our walking along the sandy beach and continued to arch again and again in shallow water, but it never swam ahead of us. It was as if no one else saw that dolphin! Then, as suddenly as the dolphin appeared to us, she was gone. I felt sad, but how could I feel sad when I was looking out at the beautiful ocean? The thought that popped into my mind was, "Come on honey, keep going. You can do it!" Something Mom always said to me in life when I was struggling, as she was my greatest cheerleader. I thought of her rooting for me as holy whispers. It was a magnificent experience to see the dolphin so close to us and a wonderful memory of my mother, Jone Anderson.

Or could that dolphin have been Mom?

———————————————

"Rejoice with those who rejoice, weep with those who weep."

Romans 12:15, ESV

"Sing for joy O Heavens, and exult, O earth; break forth, O mountains, into singing! For the Lord has comforted his people and will have compassion on his afflicted."

Isaiah 49:13, ESV

THOUGHTS

It could have been Mom. I won't know until I am in Heaven one day. But my confusion was out of nowhere, and real, and I was at my joyful place on the beach by the ocean. So why did I feel confused? Why would I suddenly, and out of nowhere, feel confused and off-kilter? Time was definitely different. It was how it usually feels when blessed experiences are given to me by God. I know, in my dreams, my longing was to reconnect with my mother. The entire experience was truly amazing, and it has stayed with me to this day, seven years later.

CHAPTER 13

Broad Stripes and Bright Stars

JULY 2020

I
t was a Thursday, the morning of the 4th of July, to be exact. I had been grieving and missing my mother, who had died one year, four months, and three days ago. Mom had dementia, but she still knew us. She also had a broken hip, which triggered her period of not eating. Two weeks after Mom stopped eating, she died.

Mom had given me a full manila envelope years prior when I visited her at her home in Canton, South Dakota, a small town 30 miles south of Sioux Falls. She'd said, "For some time reading," as she handed the manila envelope over to me. I gave her a nod as I casually tossed the envelope in the back seat of my car, along with my winter coat, boots, and scarf, in case I ever had car trouble in the winter. The manila envelope rode there with me for over a year until one day, I got around to cleaning my car, well...sort of..... people who know me well know I never really clean my car. I had moved the manila envelope to the third shelf of my shoe rack in my bedroom closet.

A couple of years passed. I'd go into my closet several times each day to change shoes or put on or take off a warmer sweater. I'd noticed that legal envelope sitting there, but I never SAW it until this morning! I saw and felt a sudden wave of shock as if I'd been struck and couldn't quite regain my balance, unable to believe what I was seeing. Right there on my shoe rack lay that manila envelope from Mom! I felt I'd been given a huge gift from Mom as I realized it was some of her writings, but then I realized it was also an enormous blessing from God. A linking object that connected me to Mom on a day when I was grieving the loss of her.

Excitedly, I untied the bow from around the large, thick envelope and gingerly pulled out a pile of Mom's writings. I began to look through everything, reading some of her poems and others that I'd not seen before. Mom had been a ferocious writer in the 1970s. She was published 54 times in *Scope* and *The Lutheran Standard*. Then, I noticed a smaller manila envelope within the stack of her writings. I carefully opened the small, tattered envelope and pulled out a booklet that had published one of Mom's poems in 1969, *Farm and Merchant Magazine*. The booklet was opened to her poem, "Broad Stripes and Bright Stars." It was a 4th of July poem! I set the booklet down and put my face in my hands. I laughed and laughed and said, "Mama, you are giving me something to laugh about even now though you are dead!" I am old enough to know there are no such things as coincidences, and even if there were, this would have been a very odd coincidence for sure. But I felt without a doubt in my mind and heart, this was from God, blessing me with a 4th of July poem written by Mom in 1969, and on one of the days I missed her and needed to hear from her! Today of all days! The 4th of July 2019 was the day I found her 4th of July poem from 1969 and I still can't fathom it!

I believe God has a sense of humor, and He knew that as my heart cried out for my mother, I needed to be comforted. God also gave me a good laugh!

A Time For Everything

"For everything there is a season, and a time for every matter under heaven. A time to be born, and a time to die; a time to plant, and a time to pluck up what is planted; a time to kill, and a time to heal; a time to break down, and a time to build up; a time to weep, and a time to laugh; a time to mourn, and a time to dance; a time to cast away stones, and a time to gather stones together; a time to embrace, and a time to refrain from embracing; a time to seek, and a time to lose; a time to keep, and a time to cast away; a time to tear and a time to sew; a time to keep silence, and a time to speak; a time to love, and a time to hate; a time for war, and a time for peace."

Ecclesiates 3, ESV

Here is my mother's poem:

"Go ahead,
America,
Wave your flag!
Cheer!
Don't be ashamed
Of the catch in your throat
when "Old Glory"
mounts the breeze.
Your flag is a symbol
of your freedom-
Freedom to read a newspaper,
write a letter,
to camp beside a mountain stream;
Freedom to worship,
work,
to walk a protest
through prejudice-breeding places.
There are those
who would tear down
America's greatness.
You be a builder-
American.
There are those
who would alienate her people
one from another.
You be a reconciler-
American.
There are those who shout ugliness,

hatred for her heroes,
her concepts,
and government.
You be a defender-
American.
Love your country.
Safeguard her future
with your best efforts,
and your prayers.
Go ahead
and wave your flag.
Wave it proudly
You are an American!"

by Jone Anderson

"Live as people who are free, not using your freedom as a cover-up for evil, but living as servants of God."

1 Peter 2:16, ESV

Thoughts

I believe God has a sense of humor. God made human beings in His image, and we humans have a sense of humor, so why wouldn't God have a sense of humor also? It is my belief that God joyfully laughs when His children are happy and laughing. I believe God celebrates our good cheer with us. I share this belief for the opposite end of the spectrum as well. I believe God grieves with His children when we are struggling with bereavement or any kind of loss. The loss of a child or a spouse, the loss of a limb or a job, the loss of a best friend who has Alzheimer's, the loss of innocence, and the loss of oneself.

When Jesus was on this earth, He too had emotions. A quick perusal through even one of the Gospels, Matthew, reveals many of these. Jesus appeared surprised when his earthly parents thought he was lost, and he was simply in his 'Father's House' talking with the leaders there. He demonstrated great compassion as he ministered to great crowds of people, healing all who came to him. For someone to be sleeping in a boat while the wind and waves tossed about and also exhorting his disciples not to worry about anything seems to indicate he felt great peace.

There was a generosity about Jesus as he invited all who were weary to come and receive from him and delight to bless the little children when they came. Impatience when he encountered faithlessness. Kindness when he responded to his mother's request and a family's need, turning water into wine at the wedding. He expressed amazement at a Roman officer's faith. He spoke with gratitude when a woman broke an expensive jar of perfume and, in his words, prepared him for burial. And Jesus showed continued patience with his disciples when they were trying to understand what he was trying to teach them.

Jesus demonstrated anger with the priests and teachers of the law for pretending to act on behalf of God when they were not themselves following God's heart. He was furious to see God's house be a place of personal financial gain when it was to be a house of prayer.

We read of Jesus lamenting that Jerusalem would not receive all he came to give and longing to 'gather them' to him as a 'hen gathers her chicks'. And of course, he felt anguish and deep distress as he prayed to his Father in heaven for a way other than the cross. Though Jesus knew it was written, the humiliation in his final day as people spat on him, stripped him of his clothes, and mocked him had to be more real than we can ever imagine. Finally, Jesus felt forsaken as he hung on the cross.

CHAPTER 14

"Will You Call the Police for Me?"

SEPTEMBER 2024

I n September 2024, a Native American man approached me in the mall parking lot in Sioux Falls, South Dakota.

I saw him out of the corner of my eye, moving towards me cautiously, yet I felt like I was watching a movie in slow motion as the Native man crouched and slowly approached me. He quietly asked, "Will you help me?" But I could hardly hear him. "What?" I replied, wanting to hear. "You want me to help you?" He nodded then and moved a bit closer to me; he was carrying a small blue case. I thought it looked like a gun case, but what did I know? "What can I do for you?" I warmly asked in my own naive way. The parking lot was jammed packed; the movie continued, as the thin, gaunt man moved closer. He spoke softly as he looked downward. His long dark hair was matted, and his clothes were dirty, as if he had slept in them out-doors for a month. I was aware of my calmness, as if watching a nice, easy-going movie, minus the popcorn. My smile was sincere, and I wanted to help this man. I stepped closer. We were alone at this part of the parking lot. The nearest folks were 120 feet from us, getting in and out of their cars to wander through the stores.

"I want to do this right," he said. "I have two warrants out for my arrest, and I want to do this right. I have a gun," he said, as he moved the blue case forward, "but I don't want to hurt anybody," he said, looking over his right shoulder towards the mall as the swell of people mosied in and out of the shops. The parking lot had been packed when my dear friend, Mary, and I drove in search of a park-ing spot. I finally found a spot way down at the south entrance of the mall, and we walked our way north to the opposite end of the mall. It was a lovely fall day, and no one wore coats or jackets. In the store, I had found a scenic picture that would go into my guest bed-room beautifully. I wanted to buy it, but a woman held the picture in her hand. Then she put the picture down, walking away from it, but she turned back and picked the picture up again. I kept my distance as this was repeated three times over 15 minutes before she finally walked away and left the picture in the store. I walked over to it, picked it up, and continued to the check-out. I was elated that I got that picture! It matched a pillow that I had on the bed in my guest room. We were leaving the store and walking through the large parking lot towards the far south entrance, where my car was, when the man first approached.

"I don't want to hurt anyone," the man said again. "Will you call the police for me?" he asked. "Sir," I asked, "you want me to call the police for you?" I clarified. He nodded yes, and I took this opportunity to remove my phone from my purse and enter 911. Mary began to talk with him as I was calling the police. "You're doing the right thing," Mary spoke softly. "This may be the hardest thing you do, but you're doing the right thing," she exclaimed. The man stood listening to her. He leaned forward and placed the blue case on the rocks surrounding a tree. Suddenly, a kid on a bicycle was at the man's side. "Now who is this?" Mary asked joyfully! This part cracked me up as there we were, talking to a man with a gun, and Mary is joyful! You have to know Mary! She is always upbeat and has always been known as "Little Mary Sunshine," coined to her in her childhood by her mother. She is consistently the happiest person I've ever known! The man said the boy was his son, but the son took off after his father spoke to him. Mary and I saw a police car pull up, and the policeman stepped out of his vehicle.

I believed we had successfully de-escalated the incident as more people had moved in closer to us than there initially were. The man remained calm as the officer searched his pants pockets, which were empty. The retired Mental Health Worker and Social Worker came alive within me, and I spoke to the policeman now. I said, "As his advocate, I want you to know that at no time was he frightening or threatening to us. It was his idea that I call you, which I did. He's trying to do the right thing by turning himself in." The native man kept his head down. The policeman nodded. "Good luck to you!" Mary hollered after him as the officer placed him in the backseat of his police car. "I'll pray for you," we said in unison. Then, the officer walked to the blue case that had a gun inside. The policeman opened the blue case, and Mary and I gasped in disbelief, "It's empty!" The officer put the blue case in his patrol car. Another patrol car pulled up, and a policewoman took Mary's and my information. Then the policeman and the policewoman left in their police cars.

The incident for us was now over. Mary and I looked at each other and let out a unified sigh! "You know, Mary, I've been praying to God to use me as I'm a helper, and I needed to help someone." "How could you be so calm?" she asked. "I don't know," I replied. "I believe it was the Spirit of God," I said softly.

"Defend the weak and the fatherless; uphold the cause of the poor and the oppressed."

Psalm 82:3

"Whoever oppresses the poor shows contempt for their Maker, but whoever is kind to the needy honors God."

Proverbs 14:31

"Speak up for those who cannot speak for themselves, for the rights of all who are destitute. Speak up and judge fairly: defend the rights of the poor and needy."

Proverbs 31:8-9

THOUGHTS

What is so interesting to me was the timing of this experience. The time in the store, the timing as we walked through the parking lot. Had the man been waiting for someone he felt safe with? My friends claim that another person might have run away from him or slugged him. Would he have run again? No answers for this experience. The man was there. Mary and I were there. We spoke. I used my phone.

The police came. The man was taken away. Both Mary and I pray for this man nightly, hoping his tomorrows are better than his yesterday's. He is God's child.

Another part of this experience that I observed within myself was that I had to have that picture! I felt as though my competitive and materialistic nature came forward in spite of being just moments away from having a spiritual experience! For I am human, and my humanness showed up! I find it challenging to be an instrument of peace, goodwill, and harmony when my human desires are right there at the top of my human self.

Epilogue

That night at Nemo's bedside when she died, I felt a sliver of God's heavenly love for His children, and I fell in love with Jesus. We've all heard people say when complaining about an illness or such, "Well, it's better than the alternative" (meaning death), but I don't share that belief. Eternal life in Heaven is far better than anything on Earth. I believe death is not fully understood on earth. We are so focused and distracted by the things of this world. Our journey is to be born again into Heaven, just as we will be born into our Heavenly Father one day. As we take our last human breath on the Earth, our next breath will be with Jesus in paradise.

As I spend time in the Bible reading God's holy word, I find the words become more than just words on a page. In fact, the words are inviting, soft, restful, comforting, and peaceful. Figuratively speaking, I can lie my head down upon God's words and feel quenched and complete, full of God's love and graciousness. To feel God's love is difficult to explain and superior to any human kind of love. For me, feeling God's love comes with tears of joy and an internal happiness that is far beyond my ability to understand or comprehend. To feel God's love has been the truest treasure of my life. I know God loves me, but have I felt the enormity of His love for me on a daily basis? No, I have not. Because that's where faith comes in! God has shown me such great care and a personal love for me in these benedictions. I know that God is always there, every second of every day, loving me, always tending His children. God shows Himself to us in these wonderful moments that are always there, if we seek Him. It seems significant to say that God, in His Holy Word, the Bible, tells us to remember who He is and what He can do. To remember the Bible stories and our own personal stories so we can tell our children and grandchildren what great works God has done for us in our lifetimes. Yes, God tells us to remember Him and to pass our stories about how much God loves us from one generation to the next. But if God were to grant me spiritual experiences every moment of everyday life, I'd have to hole up in my house, as I'd be continuously bawling my eyes out for the sheer joy that is Jesus.

It is my hope that my spiritual memoir will be helpful to you. My spiritual experiences have saved me as I navigate my way through this human life, listening for those quiet nudges that are the Holy Spirit's way of leading us toward something good. For only good comes from God, Jesus, and the Holy Spirit. May God bless us as we move closer to Him on our way through this earthly life to our everlasting home with Jesus in heaven.

This memoir is a miracle in itself! I never, ever thought I would write a book. I never thought I had anything to say! But here we are. I've said all I have. I have prayed to God, and I have decided every penny that I make from the sale of this book will go towards "Feeding South Dakota." It is wrong for me to make any money from the benedictions given to me. I have been blessed by them. These benedictions are a gift to my heart and soul. They have held me up in times of trouble, and they have blessed me to become the person that I am today.

I pray this book will be enough to have spoken to you in some small way. I pray this memoir will pique your curiosity, and you will want to seek out Jesus for yourself. Remember, only good things come from God, Jesus, and the Holy Spirit, not the bad stuff. That is just life in this broken world we live in. Jesus brings hope! Jesus brings joy!

Remember, we can choose eternal life. This earth isn't the end for Christians; life eternal in heaven is where Christians will spend all of eternity. If you accept Jesus as God's son and your Lord and Savior who died on the cross for you, for the forgiveness of your sins, then yes, you, too, will receive forgiveness of your sins, and you, too, can have eternal life in heaven.

Be vulnerable with Jesus and try to surrender to Him. He already knows all of your thoughts, actions, and sins. Be vulnerable in turning to Him in your prayers and asking for forgiveness. Seek Him and He will seek you (Jeremiah 29:13). Jesus loves you!

I'm not a preacher. I'm not a speaker. I am not a teacher. Perhaps I am to tell you these things that happened to me because it is God's will for my life, and I am just trying to be a faithful servant. Perhaps this book is for you to decide, or struggle with, for you to make up your own mind if you will choose to believe in Jesus or decide not to believe in Jesus. I'm not trying to convince you. To believe or not, that is your personal decision.

May God bless us as we move closer to Him on our way through this earthly life to our everlasting home in heaven with Him.

As my life goes on, it is time to choose, and I choose Jesus. I choose Jesus every day!

I pray you are curious, for I am just an ordinary woman.

BENEDICTION

"May the Lord bless you and keep you. May the Lord make his face to shine upon you and be gracious to you, may the Lord lift up his countenance upon you and give you peace."

Numbers 6:24-26, ESV

"Ultimately, you write what you can,
what God gives you."

Flannery O'Conner*

Citations

Epitaph

Hammarskjöld, Dag. *Markings.* Translated by Leif Sjöberg and W. H. Auden, Alfred A. Knopf, 1964.

Chapter One

Pachelbel, Johann. *Canon in D Major.* 1680-1706.

Chapter Three

Lyte, Henry Francis. *Abide with Me.* 1847.

Anderson, Joan Wester. *Where Angels Walk: True Stories of Heavenly Visitors.* Paul & Co Pub Consortium, 1992.

Chapter Four

American Psychiatric Association. *Diagnostic and Statistical Manual of Mental Disorders: DSM-IV-TR.* 4th ed., text rev., American Psychiatric Association, 2000.

Perls, Frederick S. *Gestalt Therapy Verbatim*. Real People Press, 1969.

Chapter Nine

"Everyday Meditations: Hope in God the Creator." *SpiritualDirection.com*, Sophia Institute Press, 5 Jan. 2022, spiritualdirection.com/2022/01/05/everyday-meditations-hope-in-god-the-creator.

Chapter Thirteen

Anderson, Jone. "Broad Stripes and Bright Stars." *Scope*, vol. 9, July 1969, pp. 4–5.

Anderson, Jone. "Really Friends, Hey?" *The Lutheran Standard*, vol. 8, no. 24, 26 Nov. 1968, p. 17.

Farm and Merchant Magazine, 1969.

Closing Epigraph

This quote is an amalgamation of ideas expressed in O'Connor's works such as; *The Habit of Being* and *Mystery and Manners*.

Acknowledgement

Lehn, Arianne Braithwaite. *Ash & Starlight Second Edition*. Chalice Press, 3

Oct. 2023.

ACKNOWLEDGEMENTS

Becky Ekeland: A dear friend who read the earliest versions of this manuscript 30+ years ago. Thank you for your time in reading that grammatically awful first draft and for the years of friendship and support. You are a gem!

The Writers Group: Mary Alice Haug, our fearless leader, published author, and retired college professor, thank you for your expertise and for inviting me to be a part of the writers' group. I loved every minute of it!

Patricia Fishback: A retired Social Worker and writer, thank you for reading my manuscript and for all your grammar work.

Mary Husman: A former English teacher and writer of a book on autism, thank you for all your generous help with grammar.

Lewayne Erickson: Attorney and fellow seeker of the truth. Thank you for listening to my stories.

Maree Larson: Chairwoman of the Larson Foundation and writer, thank you for your gentle spirit and for keeping my secret.

Mildred "Millie," Juel: Writer, concert pianist and singer, and a friend who knew my grandma, Nemo! Thank you for sharing your-self with me and your feedback while writing my spiritual memoir.

Paula Tursam: Retired Special Education Teacher and writer, thank you for all your good ideas!

Lynette Olson: Retired teacher of English and Music and writer, thank you for your gentle suggestions, plus all your help with grammar work.

In Memory of Kathryn Quinones: An enthusiastic writer who provided me with helpful feedback.

In Memory of: Pricilla Eitel: A gifted 90-year-old writer, harp player, and a gentle soul who danced in her kitchen. Thank you for your tender spirit and listening.

Sandra Ballou: a writer and a helpful listener.

In Memory of my Mom, Jone Anderson: Oblate, a writer of 54 published articles in the 70's in Scope and The Lutheran Standard. Former Hospice worker, wife and mother of three, grandmother and great-grandmother. Thank you for everything. I will always love you and my memories.

Tacey Eneboe-Braithwaite: Attorney, wife, mother, grand-mother, brave widow, and dear friend of 65 years, for reading my manuscript and for helping me find scriptural passages. I love you, my dear childhood friend who suffers from Alzheimer's Disease. I hold our memories for both of us.

Arianne Braithwaite Lehn: Minister with the Presbyteri-an Church (USA), Artist, Creator, Author of *Ash and Starlight: Prayers for the Chaos and Grace of Daily Life*, wife and mother of three children. Thank you for reading my manuscript as a woman and as a pastor. And for your written words on my website. (Daughter of Tacey Braithwaite.)

Gloria Houle: Retired Social Worker and dear friend of 50 years. You are a sister to me. Thank you for your reading, positive feedback, and your belief in me. I love you.

Jean Bearden: My heart rejoices at having you as my dear friend. I've always seen Jesus in your face, and I feel so blessed to have you as a mentor and someone I look to when I have life concerns and Biblical questions. A million thank-you's for all your support, help, and prayers that you have blessed me with in my life and since the writing of this book! I'm very grateful you walked this path with me. It was quite a season! God bless you always, Jean, and I love you.

In Memory of Dr. Marie J. DiSciullo-Naples: Ph.D., SB Oblate and Spiritual Director. Thank you for all your insight, for poring over the manuscript with a fine-tooth comb, and for writing the foreword to this book. I will always remember you!

Gale Gor: Trusted friend, good listener, and wise woman who heard my fears about publishing and gave me the courage to be myself and go forward in an attempt to publish. It was a pivotal conversation for me, a God thing, and you became my therapist! Thank you. You are a true friend, and I love you!

Pat Rogne: Thank you, Pat, for reading my manuscript and being so willing and helpful in sharing your feedback with me. Thank you also for your loving friendship that goes back to our college days at Augustana University in Sioux Falls, South Dakota. You are a true friend and I love you!

Leah Gedstad Hoem: My dear daughter, who came to my beck

and call to practice Zoom with me, reading and rereading my manuscript. Thank you for your help with grammar and punctuation and for your support in this endeavor. Love you always, Sweetie!

Lily Murray: to my granddaughter and her best friend and college roommate, Ryann Davis, who helped me with Zoom, ClickUp, emotional support, and for the wonderful conversation! Thank you, my dear women! Love you both!

Carol Sommer: Neighbor and friend. Thank you for trying to help me with Zoom, and sorry you had to witness my technological meltdowns. Thank you, Carol!

Marcia Sogn Knutson: I'm so happy to be reconnected with you! Thank you for reading my manuscript and for sharing your Christian concerns with me. Thank you to your Bible Study group, who prayed for me.

Dr. Douglas Anderson: PsyD in Clinical Psychology, MA in Clinical Psychology, MA in Counseling, MDiv. I owe you my life! Thank you for being my therapist 27 years ago and for walking with me through my depression and divorces, and for walking with me now, as a friend, in reading my manuscript. For your insight, your respect and kindness to me, thank you.

Merrick Anderson: My great niece. Thank you from the bottom of my heart for answering my cry for help with five simple words, "Of course I can help!" After four months of floundering, I was ready to quit hope*writers. I even made a declaration to them that I was quitting! Then, in prayer, Merrick's name came into my mind. God led me to call Merrick! Your research on understanding ClickUp was amazing, and your help with everything is way beyond my simple words of "thank you!" Without your help, there wouldn't be a published Benediction Given. I love you!

Donna Rolsma, Jody Kusek, and Deb Teunissen: Thank you for the feedback and support of me, for reading my manuscript, and for your friendship! I love you guys!

Lois Sayre: A dear woman who lived across the street from me when my first child was little. Lois helped give me confidence as a young mother and spent time with my child, so I was able to rest. Thank you for reading my manuscript and word clarification. I have always loved you, my dear friend. Lois is also the author of a beautiful book on Oscar Howe.

I could not have accomplished my goal to publish without the help of some very special individuals with hope*books: Hope Dover, Mary Gleason, Casey Winchester, Lauren Scott, Angela Abbott, Kati Benton, Jennifer Beasley, and Carrie Watts.

Paige Fiegen: Thank you for all your help with grammar and punctuation! You and Merrick are my little angels, and I don't know what I'd have done without you both and all your technological skills.

My attorney: Rory King of Bantz, Gosch & Cremer L.L.C. in Aberdeen, South Dakota. For research and reading through my contract. Your help gave me peace of mind.

Wendy Stein with Bantz, Gosch, & Cremer L.L.C. in Aberdeen, South Dakota. For your gentle kindness to me when I was struggling to get the contract to you. I felt your care, and that meant the world to me in those early days of technological frustration and tears.

For my person who is too humble to be recognized for his/her insights, suggestions, and reading and re-reading my spiritual memoir. You know who you are! A heartfelt thank-you, and you know I love you.

In memory of my father, O.L. "Larry" Anderson, for reading my manuscript and for your continued support, I carry on with this book in telling my story. And for your suggestions that I include a 'thoughts" paragraph after every spiritual experience. My father was an anchor for me. I love you, Dad.

www.ingramcontent.com/pod-product-compliance
Lightning Source LLC
Chambersburg PA
CBHW031421120626
46545CB00006B/2209